CHRISTIAN

HELPING YOURSELF AND OTHERS

TO LIVE BIBLICALLY

KEITH DORRICOTT

Copyright © Keith Dorricott 2014

CONTENTS

(D) Particular Situations

- How to Resolve Conflict
- How to Help in a Crisis
- Marital Counseling
- Pre-marital Counseling

1. AN INTRODUCTION TO PART ONE

The first man Adam was made in the image of God (Gen.1:27). He could think, feel and make choices. He could relate to God, who is spirit, and to other humans. While he had a physical body, he also had a soul and a spirit (1 Thess.5:23). He was made for a purpose – to relate to God and to glorify God. He was a perfect human being.

But, also like his creator, he had a free will, and by it he disobeyed the one restriction placed on him. By that sin he "fell" into depravity and his faculties became flawed. While he had originally been formed by God, now he became deformed by sin. Later Adam begot a son after his image (Gen.5:3), and in this way the human race has ensued down through the centuries – made for God, but with the faculties for doing so impaired, with a bias for evil.

But God in His Son has been working towards the restoration of fallen mankind to the divine image. Christ came as a perfect and sinless man into this world, the perfect revelation of the person of God. Through His sacrificial death God is now justifying individuals by faith, then sanctifying them throughout their lives, until He will finally glorify them. His purpose is that they should be conformed to the image of His perfect Son (Rom.8:29).

And so the purpose of God for believers in this life is our 'sanctification' – being made holy. While our justification takes only a moment, our sanctification is a lifelong work. This sanctification is a continuously being drawn closer to God in Christ, to reflect the glory of God, through the work of the Holy Spirit within us. It is a drawing away from sinful acts and influences into a deeper experience of God and likeness to Him, so as to work out His purpose and will in our lives.

The experiences of our lives, many of which are not pleasant, have this as their objective – spiritual and personal maturity.

"Now may the God of peace ... make you complete in every good work to do His will, working in you what is well pleasing in His sight, through Jesus Christ." (Heb.13:20-21)

All human problems have at their root sin in this world, although not necessarily the sin of the individuals involved. If we are to properly understand ourselves and others, why we do what we do, why we feel the way we do, we need to first understand how God has made us and what has gone wrong (see chapter 2). Only then can we be restored to the path of fulfillment which God has set out for us, and which Christ described as the "abundant life" (Jn.10:10).

Part I of this book helps us to help ourselves, a process which begins with an attempt to understand ourselves. We need to look at the built-in personal needs that we all have (see chapter 3), and which we constantly try to meet, either consciously or unconsciously. Then we examine the goals we set for ourselves (see chapter 3) – what we aim at because we think (rightly or wrongly), that by achieving them we will have these essential needs met. We will see how easily we can have misguided goals. Then we will see how our actions and conduct are the result of choices we make, again consciously or unconsciously, by which we intend to meet these goals (see chapter 5).

And we will see how failure to meet the goals or fulfill our needs brings about negative emotions – we feel unhappy. And so we have a problem – either an individual difficulty or a problem in a relationship with one or more other people. Underlying all this is our thinking, our assumptions, what we believe to be true about how to achieve our goals and meet our needs (see chapter 4). We will learn that when we change our thinking, which is not easy to do, we will inevitably change our behaviour and the way we feel about our circumstances (see chapters 6-11).

Part II explores the process of how we can help others as well as ourselves (using of course what has been learned in Part 1, which will apply to them as it did to us). In all of this, the work of God and the Word of God must be paramount. To do otherwise is to disclaim the very power and purpose which is the basis of the solution we seek.

Correcting the problems that become apparent to us, such as those discussed in Part 1, is often not easy to do, because it often involves a fundamental change in deeply held beliefs. Most problems develop over a period of time. Generally, the earlier that assistance is provided, the better the opportunity will be to help bring about necessary change. However, problems can often progress to an advanced stage before a person is willing to admit they could use some help. As a rule, that makes it harder to be of real help.

Some people who come for counseling have a problem with undisciplined living – due to lack of structure and purpose in their lives. They tend to follow their feelings instead of making deliberate choices and sticking to them. They need to be given ways to remind themselves of their obligations, to make plans and commitments, to set deadlines and schedules, and to adhere to them no matter how they feel. They may need to have someone who can hold them accountable.

A counselor can suggest ways how they may do these things, and then monitor their progress in them. When people feel least like pursuing the process is generally when they need it the most. No one, including a counselor, can bring about a change in another person. All of us can only change ourselves. We will change when we are sufficiently motivated to do so - perhaps when the present state of affairs becomes bad enough, and when we truly believe it is for our good.

2. UNDERSTANDING WHO WE ARE AS HUMANS

The human functions of beliefs, feelings and behaviour relate directly to the three functions of a person's essential being, which the Bible refers to as our soul. Beliefs (including thinking, understanding, assumptions, attitudes and values) relate to our mind. Feelings relate to our emotions. And behaviour results from the exercise of our will. The mind, emotions and the will are the three core functions of the soul.

But as humans we have more than a soul. We also have a body (and so are physical beings) and we have a spirit (and so are spiritual beings). We know about our body the most, due to medical science. The body can be observed, photographed and X-rayed, whereas the soul and the spirit are invisible.

a. Our Human Body

We know how our body comes into being – through reproduction. From conception it contains within itself the seed of sin (Ps.51:5), which is received from our father (which is why Christ had to be "the seed of the woman" only). From an early age this sin infiltrates our soul (mind, emotions, will) and even our human spirit (2 Cor.7:1). This prompts sinful behaviour. Therefore all "fleshly" behaviour has its root in the power of sin in our body. This is why Paul referred to "the body of sin" (Rom.6:6), and "this body of death" (Rom.7:24). For us to live "spiritually", we have to put our body in subjection and not allow sin to control ("reign in") it. Even in a believer "the body is dead because of sin" (Rom. 8:10). It is susceptible to disease and affliction, and is mortal.

When we receive eternal life at the moment of our salvation, our body does not become saved, even though the Spirit of God takes up residence within it. It continues to plague us as a source of fleshly lusts unless it is subdued and its influence replaced by the enabling power of God through our spirit. The body dies when the spirit (the life force) leaves it. At its resurrection it will be replaced by a glorified body from heaven (a "spiritual body") that is not mortal or sinful. This is referred to as the redemption of our body (Rom.8:23).

b. Our Human Spirit

Our spirit is an individual creation of God; He is "the Father of spirits" (Heb.12:9). Our spirit enters our body at birth, it seems, when we become independently living beings. It is our spirit that enables us to communicate with God, our creator, who is spirit (Jn.4:24). This communication takes place with God the Holy Spirit (Rom.8:16). There are three core functions of the human spirit also. These are:

(a) revelation (the ability to know God and the things of God as the Spirit of God enlightens us – Prov.20:27);

(b) communion (the ability to worship, praise and pray to God through the Holy Spirit – 1 Cor.14:15; Phil.3:3)); and

(c) conscience (the ability to discern right and wrong, as convicted by the Holy Spirit – Rom.9:1).

Spiritual death takes place when we as a child become accountable for their wrong actions, which are the inevitable outcome of the sin force ("the law of sin") within our bodies. The connection between our spirit and the Holy Spirit becomes severed. At the new birth, however, they are re-connected and the Holy Spirit takes up residence to become a permanent part of our on-going functioning. As a new believer we now have two conflicting sources of influence into our souls – the old fleshly lusts from our body ("which war against their soul" - 1 Pet.2:11), and the Spirit of God through our spirit. It is our regenerated spirit that is the new creature that cannot sin (1 Jn.3:9). However, it is up to our will (in our soul) to decide which will predominate in us – whether we will be carnal or spiritual. Spiritual maturity is where the Spirit is dominating – our mind thinks and believes the things of God, our emotions experience the fruit of the Spirit, and our will consciously chooses what is in accord with the will of God. Finally, at death, our spirit departs our body and returns to God who gave it (Ecc.12:7), to be reunited with our soul and our glorified body at resurrection.

c. Our Human Soul

Thirdly, our soul is also a unique creation (Jer.38:16) which, it seems, comes into existence at the union of spirit and body at birth (Gen.2:7). It is our soul that sins as a conscious act of the will (Ezek.18:4), and therefore is condemned to eternal punishment. But our soul can be eternally saved by a conscious act of our will to subject itself to the will of God – by exercising faith to salvation. This intervention changes its destiny after death to heaven, to be with Christ. Our mind, emotions and will are not immediately transformed when we first put faith in Christ. This is a life-long process, and is the essence of on-going sanctification. The full salvation of our mind, emotions and will takes place at the rapture when we will be conformed to the image of the Son of God, to which we have been pre-destined (Rom.8:29). It is this on-going salvation of our souls (our beliefs, our feelings and our behaviour) that we are concerned about here.

"... at the revelation of Jesus Christ ... receiving the end of your faith - the salvation of your souls" (1 Pet.1:7-9).

(Editor's note: See chapter 1 of Keith's book "Our Spiritual Journey" for a more detailed look at the body, soul and spirit).

3: UNDERSTANDING OUR PERSONAL NEEDS AND GOALS

All of us as human beings have fundamental personal needs that must be met. Until they are, we cannot function effectively and all our behaviour will be motivated towards meeting them. This is sometimes referred to as "deficit motivation" - we are motivated to make up the deficit. (Like a bank overdraft, we can't start paying out until we have put enough in to cover the overdraft.) Expecting someone with unmet needs to live responsibly before God is like asking someone with laryngitis to speak up. We are not intended to live according to God's plan without first being equipped with God's provisions to do so.

When these personal needs are met, we are freed to be able to give of ourselves, to love unconditionally and therefore to live productive and happy lives. We can then fulfill the two "great commandments": "You shall love the LORD your God with all your heart, with all your soul, and with all your mind"; and "You shall love your neighbor as yourself" (Matt.22:37-40).

This is personal spiritual maturity.

Security and Significance

Our personal needs can be broadly divided into two categories: Security - our need to feel truly and unconditionally loved, accepted and safe; to belong; and Significance - our need to feel important and worthwhile, to have purpose and meaning in our life, usually involving having made a substantial and lasting impact on others.

When people have been asked to reflect on what they really want and long for in their life, these are the two things that have emerged. When either or both of these fundamental needs are met at any particular mo-

9

ment, we feel an inner sense of vitality and wholeness, and our energy level is higher. We feel whole.

Security

Security is a convinced awareness of being totally and unconditionally loved without needing to change or do anything in order to get that love. The love and acceptance is not earned and therefore cannot be lost. The opposite of acceptance is rejection, which can be painful. Fear of rejection is one of the strongest human fears. Insecurity can greatly impair our relationships, because it leads to fear that others might not relate to us as we want. Examples of this unconditional love in scripture include:

- Paul's expressions of the love of Christ (Rom.8:35; Eph.3:19);
- Job's yearning to see his redeemer (19:25-27);
- John's exclamation of the Father's love (1 Jn.3:1); and
- Ruth's love for Naomi (1:16,17).

Christians may feel that they don't love the Lord enough. What they need instead is to realize how much the Lord loves them. Love begets love; His love is what fosters our love in return. Our security is not in what we do for Him, but in Him personally. It's all about our relationship with Him. Our identity must be in God.

"... the glory of His grace, by which He has made us accepted in the Beloved" (Eph.1:6).

"Receive one another, just as Christ also received us, to the glory of God" (Rom.15:7,8).

Significance

Significance is a realization that we are engaged in a responsibility or task that is truly important, whose results will not evaporate over time but will last, that involves having a meaningful impact on another person, and for which we are completely adequate. It gives us hope, which we all need. We all have longings, but we may turn to various means to have them met. The opposite of significance is indifference, emptiness and hopelessness.

Examples from scripture of people whose purpose in life gave them a sense of significance and motivated them to great things include:

- Abraham's willingness to leave his homeland to find the city of God (Heb.11:9,10);
- Jeremiah's motivation to endure endless persecution because he knew his mission for God (Jer.20:9); and
- Paul's willingness to defer his entrance to heaven to fulfill his ministry (Phil.1:21-4).

Their purpose in life gave them significance. It is important that we acknowledge our longings so that we can examine them to see if they are well placed.

Generally, security needs tend to be somewhat stronger in women (hence their desire for relationships), and significance needs tend to be stronger in men (thus the importance of their careers; many men measure their worth by what they accomplish). However, these generalizations are not always the case. This difference is perhaps traceable to the first couple on earth, and why each was created. Adam was created to fulfill God's purpose on the earth (Is.43:7). Eve was subsequently created for Adam (1 Cor.11:9), because it wasn't good for him to be alone (Gen.2:18).

How Are Our Needs Met?

These needs were placed in us by God Himself, and they can only be fully and permanently met by Him. We have been made for God. If we try to have them met by other people or other means, we will eventually fall and be disappointed. Worldly rewards may satisfy us for a short time, but they soon lead to a desire for more. This becomes an endless cycle or treadmill.

We do not need to actually 'feel' secure or significant in order to function effectively. We are responsible to believe the Word of God when it tells us that we are in fact secure in His love and that we are a significant part of His plans. Christ Himself has made us secure and significant. As believers we are "in Christ"; whether we feel it or not, it is true. The more we choose to live according to the truth of what Christ has done for us, and is doing for us, the more we will come to actually sense the reality of our security and significance in Him. When instead we look for these needs to be met by other people, as is a common tendency, we are in effect giving them the power to withhold them from us, and thus defeat us, which dooms us to failure.

> *"It is better to trust in the LORD than to put confidence in man"* (Ps.118:8).

Dependence or Independence?

God created us in His image, as dependent beings. He 'is' love (security) and He 'has' a purpose (significance). We in turn need love and we need purpose. This need for love and purpose are intended to be fulfilled by God. It was the result of man's fall that these needs can remain unmet. It is independence from God which initiated sin in the first place and which continues to result in unhappy and ruined lives. The sinful soul does not like to feel helpless; it wants to be in control. Many times, we may seek to survive without relying on God. We need instead to be convinced of the complete goodness of God, and so have full confidence in Him. The only remedy is to return to a dependence on God, through faith.

This is accomplished through first experiencing the salvation which God provides through Christ, and then living in the power of that life of God that we have received. Much activity, even of Christians, is (consciously or unconsciously) motivated to gain someone else's approval and acceptance. When we don't meet what we think are their expectations, we can feel guilty. But this is based on flawed thinking.

As interdependent persons, we cannot function without close relationships with other people. In fact, relationships involve the deepest part of our human personality. These needs relate to our soul, our person, quite separate from our body. They are not reducible to biological or chemical analysis, as humanists claim. Because we are social beings who seek these relationships, many of our problems in life relate to conflicts with other people.

Ignoring our personal needs can be dangerous and destructive. Just as failure to meet our physical needs results in physical deterioration and death, so failure to meet our personal needs results in decreasing personal effectiveness and happiness.

Dealing with the Needs of Others

As human beings we have been made to be able to relate to each other. How we relate to each other is a reflection of how we relate to God Himself. It is a natural tendency to be taken up primarily with ourselves. God is the source of all true love to others. When our relationships are governed more by a fear of being hurt, they will be superficial and defensive. Similarly, in dealing effectively with other people, it is important to understand how their needs and characteristics affect their interactions with us.

Here are some examples:

   1. People's number one fear is rejection, generally, and their

number one need is acceptance;

2. We need to deal with people in a way that protects or enhances their self- esteem;
3. Everyone approaches any situation with some concern about "What's in it for me?";
4. Everyone naturally prefers to talk about things that are important to them personally;
5. People only hear and incorporate what they understand;
6. People like, trust and believe those who like them;
7. People often do things for other than the apparent reasons;
8. Even quality people can act petty and small at times;
9. People tend to wear a social mask; we must look beyond it to see the person.

Personal Goals

Whether we are aware of these basic personal needs or not, we translate them into specific goals that we work towards in our lives, and that motivate our actions and behaviour. The particular goals we set ourselves depend on the beliefs and assumptions that we have as to what will in fact meet our needs. To the extent that these beliefs are not true, even achieving the goals will leave the needs still unmet.

Examples of commonly-held goals that are based on untrue beliefs (and that therefore don't work) are:

- "My performance (e.g. as a husband or wife) will earn me the love and acceptance of other people (e.g. my spouse)";
- "Accumulating wealth will enable me to feel secure for later life, and be able to ensure I can provide for my family";
- "Having a successful career will make me an important person"; and
- "Having substantial possessions will give me status in other

peoples' eyes and therefore in my own eyes".

Society's culture (as promoted by the deception of the ruler of this world, the devil) encourages us to measure a person's worth by their appearance and achievements (house, social circles, status, clothing, cars, talent, etc.). It is a sad thing when these are a Christian's goals also, and it causes them to fall short of God and His glory. We may profess to rely on God and yet have "functional gods" that we rely on for our deepest satisfactions.

Many people look to have their needs met totally in human relationships. For example, there are marriages which are implicitly a mutual commitment to exploit the other person in order to fulfill personal needs. That is a recipe for failure, since no person can succeed in doing so all the time. Two people in a relationship who already have their needs met in Christ can instead concentrate on ministering to each other (to satisfy the other's desires), to please one another), rather than manipulating each other to try to have their own needs met.

Where our goals cannot be met for some reason, frustration results and can be expressed in a variety of negative feelings. If the goals themselves are unattainable, since the obstacles cannot be eliminated, the only remedy is to change the goals to something attainable. If God is not satisfying our souls, we will seek something else to satisfy us, which violates our inherent design. This is where our personal problems begin. It can also be the beginning of obsessions and compulsions. Nothing will satisfy our soul like a passionate relationship with Jesus Christ.

Goals vs. desires

Goals are different from desires, dreams or aspirations. Wanting certain things is not necessarily wrong. It is the dependence on these to meet our fundamental personal needs that are to be met by God that is misguided. We are meant to long after God, to have Christ at the centre of our lives.

> *"For to me, to live is Christ ..."* (Phil.1:21).

To be effective, a goal needs to have: (a) a definite timeline by which we intend to accomplish it; and (b) definite accountabilities along the way. Without these, it is just an aspiration. If an outcome is not within our control to attain then it is not a legitimate goal to set. It is futile for us to set goals for ourselves where we cannot determine their achievement. An example is trying to change someone else's behaviour, or holding ourselves responsible for their performance. We cannot make someone love us or treat us well. The only person we can change is ourselves - and that is hard enough. But that is a valid goal.

Changing someone else may be a desire, and we may succeed in convincing them to change themselves, but changing them should not be a goal. It will just lead to failure and frustration. What we can do is change how we react and respond to them. We are ultimately only accountable for ourselves (including how we interact with others).

4. UNDERSTANDING OUR THINKING AND BELIEFS

"With the heart a person believes" (Rom.10:10).

Beliefs are the assumptions, ideas and thinking that we are convinced are true. Our beliefs determine our actions and feelings. It is very possible to not be consciously aware of some of our beliefs and assumptions. The real test of what we truly believe is not what we say we believe, but what we actually act on.

As we grow up as children, the socialization process in the world (through parents, teachers, peers, the media, etc.) conditions us to accept certain beliefs as explanations for what leads to success in life, many of which are in fact contrary to the Word of God and therefore not true. While they may appear to work for a time, they contain fundamental flaws. Only scripture contains the absolute truth as to what leads to a fulfilled life. In this respect, the Bible is sufficient for us. This does not mean that secular knowledge is always necessarily wrong or unhelpful, but it must always be subject to the supremacy of the Word of God.

> *"His divine power has given to us all things that pertain to life and godliness, through the knowledge of Him who called us by glory and virtue"* (2 Pet.1:3).

The Power of Our Beliefs

Beliefs are very useful. Because we believe them to be true, we can apply them to a variety of situations that we face and resolve them efficiently. We seldom revisit them or challenge them with new information, and we don't spend a lot of time thinking about them. If, however, our beliefs are flawed, perhaps because they're based on assumptions that have never been tested, we can be severely limiting ourselves and setting in motion adverse behaviour, consequences and feelings. Just as having knowledge about other people helps us to predict their behaviour, having knowledge about ourselves is even more important. It helps to understand how we developed these characteristics, and why we persist in them, so that we can learn how to replace them.

Inner Dialogue

All of us have an inner dialogue; we constantly tend to talk to ourselves. This inner dialogue reflects our inner beliefs. We can convince ourselves and reinforce certain notions in our minds by repeating them to ourselves, whether they are true or not true. Psychologists say that thoughts go through our minds at the rate of 1300 words per minute. Our imaginations are very powerful, and they can have a positive or negative effect on us. If we constantly engage in negative self-talk, we cannot reasonably expect anything other than negative outcomes. Our minds are like tape recorders, and we tend to replay the tapes frequently. Our minds can get stuck in a rut, in a pattern of thinking (that may in fact be opposed to the will of God). Often what makes sense to us is wrong biblically.

"Everyone did what was right in his own eyes" (Jdg.21:25).

Reality or Perception?

We all view the world and our own experiences through filters. We interpret events and circumstances. Two people can attribute very different meanings to the same thing. It is not our circumstances, but our perception of them, that makes us happy or unhappy. We can get upset when our expectations are not met, even if those expectations are misguided. Some filters may be healthy and constructive, while others may be distorted and destructive. They are the result of things we have learned in the past. Each person's perception is unique. However, there are some common gender differences; for example, women often attach emotional significance to things that men typically don't.

Some people who have experienced great tragedies in their lives have chosen a constructive alternative in order to give some positive meaning to it. Not that they would have chosen the tragedy but, because it did happen, they chose through social action to create meaning out of it. They consciously change their perception of what happened.

Changing our perceptions usually involves understanding how they were shaped by our past, so that we can choose to not let our past dictate our future. For example, if we hold on to anger because of how someone once treated us, once we acknowledge that pain and how it has altered the way we view things, we can consciously choose to no longer be a prisoner of that perceptions. And so, once we understand our own filters, and those of other people, the resulting behaviour often makes sense. However, it is generally easier to recognize distorted filters in other people than in ourselves. Filters can become fixed limiting beliefs that we no longer adjust with new information that comes to us. We therefore need to periodically test and verify our view of the world. This is sometimes referred to as making an "attitude adjustment".

Two Inputs - Which Dominates?

For the Christian, there are two different sources of belief, which manifest themselves in our inner dialogue:

Carnal sources

These involve the combined effects of three powerful forces: (1) our own natural inner fleshly lusts, (2) what we observe and perceive in the world around us, and (3) the influence of demonic beings who, under Satan, are dedicated to destroying our spiritual lives by infiltrating our minds. These sources operate the same way in the Christian as in the non-Christian.

Spiritual Sources

As a result of our new birth, we have the Holy Spirit living within us. Through our regenerated human spirits, He communicates to us from scripture the truth of God and its meaning for us in our situation. This process depends on our willing cooperation with Him, which we give Him by our faith. It is therefore our "faith" which appropriates to us God's grace (His equipping and enabling), which is sufficient for all our needs in every situation. It is through our faith therefore that we can overcome this world and all its wrong thinking and influence, because Christ has overcome it for us (Jn.16:33; 1 Jn.5:4). At our new birth, we were each placed "in Christ", which makes available to us the full power of God - which is what is necessary to transform our lives to become truly mature, to live as God intends.

We then need to receive and apply this power in its various forms day by day "by the Spirit". Thus *"in Christ (Jesus)"* and *"in the Spirit"* are twin truths which are vital to dealing with our human problems. (For example, compare Romans 15:16 (*"sanctified in Christ Jesus"*), and 1 Corinthians 1:2 (*"sanctified by the Spirit"*). It is Christ's work that makes it possible; it is the Spirit's work to make it real to us.

Changing Our Beliefs

Romans 12:2 makes it clear that our minds (our thinking) needs to be changed if we are to be transformed into the divine image:

> *"Do not be conformed to this world, but be transformed by the renewing of your mind, so that you may prove what the will of God is, that which is good and acceptable and perfect."*

The process of moving "over" from wrong beliefs to biblical beliefs is difficult for us and requires a lot of reinforcement and support. However actually acting on a truth of scripture, as an initial act of faith, will help to convince us of its validity, and strengthen our faith in it. We cannot wait to "feel like it" or until we want to. The feelings tend to follow the new actions, rather than motivate them. It is a choice we have to make. Choosing to act on a clear word of scripture is an act of faith that activates the power of the Spirit in us to change our underlying beliefs which govern our actions.

As we progressively act on the basis that the Word of God is actually true and is applicable to the situations we face in life, our conviction of it will strengthen until we become deeply convinced of it.

"Let the words of my mouth and the meditation of my heart be acceptable in Your sight, O LORD". (Ps.19:14)

"Through Your precepts I get understanding" (Ps.119:104).

Most human problems begin in the mind. It is our wrong thinking that leads us to attitudes of self-sufficiency, pride, bitterness, and non-Christian values. That is why we need to have our minds renewed, as Romans 12:2 says. This takes place by us consciously and deliberately setting our minds on the things of the Spirit in the Word of God (Romans 8:5).

What is Faith?

Faith is a deep inner conviction that something is true, and thus is completely reliable as a basis for action. It is much more than knowing something mentally, and much more than an attitude of positive thinking. Scripture refers to it as believing with "our heart" (Rom.10:10). Faith in God is the fundamental prerequisite for any relationship with Him. Doubt and being "of two minds" is evidence of a lack of faith. Our actions are the proof of what we really believe, not what we say we believe.

"Faith is the substance of things hoped for, the evidence of things not seen" (Heb.11:1).

"Faith comes by hearing, and hearing by the word of God" (Rom.10:17).

"He who doubts is like a wave of the sea driven and tossed by the wind. For let not that man suppose that he will receive anything from the Lord; he is a double-minded man, unstable in all his ways" (Jas.1:6-8).

The Place of the Word of God in Our Thinking

The two primary spiritual resources that we have been given are (a) the Word of God; and (b) the Holy Spirit, who reveals the Word and convicts us with it. The Bible is more than a guide book to spiritual truth. Many religions claim to have such a holy book. But the Bible is unique because it reveals God. Because each word is inspired by God Himself, it is completely accurate, infallible and authoritative. It contains absolute truth which is entirely relevant for the problems we face, even centuries after it was written. We need to saturate ourselves with it, in order to have our thinking changed from the conventional thinking of this world which we passively assimilate. This is what is meant by having our minds "renewed".

When we properly understand the thinking, assumptions and beliefs which underlie our actions and feelings, we need to challenge them as to their accuracy and correctness. If they do not conform to the Word of God, taken in its proper context, then we need to change our thinking. That new thinking needs to be reinforced by acting on it until we truly "believe" it.

"You have put off the old man with his deeds and have put on the new man who is renewed in knowledge according to the image of Him who created him" (Col.3:9).

Myths and Truth

Following is a list of some commonly held beliefs and assumptions in the world, which are contrary to what scripture teaches.

Myth	Truth	Scripture
What I don't know (or can ignore) won't hurt me.	Knowing and admitting the truth will allow me to no longer be controlled by sin.	*Jn.8:31-32: "If you abide in My word, you are My disciples indeed. And you shall know the truth, and the truth shall make you free."*
The Bible doesn't help with most of life's real problems.	God has made provision for every aspect of my life.	*2 Pet.1:3: "His divine power has given to us all things that pertain to life and godliness, through the knowledge of Him who called us"*
I can't do what I should do, no matter how I try.	Nothing is expected of us by God that He doesn't equip us for.	*Phil.4:13: "I can do all things through Christ who strengthens me."*
My self-worth depends on my acceptance by other people.	My acceptance by others is unreliable; they are dealing with their own issues.	*Col.2:10: "you are complete in Him"*
I do what I think is right. No one's going to tell me what to	My view of right and wrong is based on my own perceptions. God has told me what is right and wrong.	*Jer.17:9: "The heart is deceitful above all things, And desperately wicked; Who can know it?"*

do.

I still feel guilty for what I did years ago.	Repentance and confession of sin results in forgiveness and a clean slate.	*1 Jn. 1:9: "if we confess our sins, He is faithful and just to forgive us our sins and to cleanse us from all unrighteousness."*
People will only love me if I do what they expect of me.	God loves me unconditionally. I can't earn love.	*Eph.1:6: "He has made us accepted in the Beloved"*
If I can save enough money, I will feel secure for the future.	Trusting in my wealth is hazardous; there are too many uncertainties. God has pledged to meet my needs.	*1 Tim.6:17: "Command those who are rich in this present age not to be haughty, nor to trust in uncertain riches but in the living God, who gives us richly all things to enjoy."*
I need to make something of myself in this world to be important.	My significance as a person comes from the fact that I am valued by God and am an important part of His purpose.	*2 Thess.2:13-15: "God from the beginning chose you ... for the obtaining of the glory of our Lord Jesus Christ."*
I can do it better myself. Sharing and	I need other people. God has given us varying abilities and expects us to work together.	*Rom.7:18: "in me (that is, in my flesh) nothing good dwells; for to will is present with me, but how to perform what is good I do not find."*

delegating is a bother.

I need to control how other people treat me or I might get hurt.	I can't control other people. My protection is provided by God.	Rom.8:35-37: "Who shall separate us from the love of Christ? Shall tribulation, or distress, or persecution, or famine, or nakedness, or peril, or sword? ... in all these things we are more than conquerors through Him who loved us."
I can't be happy unless I'm married.	While marriage is ordained by God, singleness allows me to dedicate myself to serve Him.	1 Cor.7:17,32: "as God has distributed to each one, as the Lord has called each one, so let him walk ... he who is unmarried cares for the things of the Lord -how he may please the Lord."
What I do in secret doesn't hurt anybody.	Everything I do has a consequence – to me, and often to others.	Rom.14:7: "none of us lives to himself, and no one dies to himself."
I don't need Christ in my life.	My satisfaction of my need for security and significance can only fully come through embracing the provision of Christ.	Jn.4:13-14: "Whoever drinks of this water will thirst again, but whoever drinks of the water that I shall give him will never thirst."
I have to look after myself in this world; nobody else will.	God has undertaken to look after me.	Matt.6:33: "seek first the kingdom of God and His righteousness, and all these things shall be added to you."

| I need to be the boss to achieve what I want done. | My greatness will come from serving others. | *Matt. 20:26: "whoever desires to become great among you, let him be your servant."* |

5. UNDERSTANDING HOW WE BEHAVE AND FEEL

"As he thinks in his heart, so is he" (Prov.23:7).

Almost all human behaviour is rational. That is, it is consistent with what the individual believes to be in their best interest, even if that belief happens to be misguided. It is motivated to achieve their goals, whether those goals are conscious or not. It is not possible to actually motivate another person. What we often refer to as motivating others is really helping them to become convinced that a certain course of action is in their own best interests. When that happens, they become self-motivated.

To illustrate how powerful this is, here are 8 Biblical examples of wrong behaviour (a) that came about because of a wrong belief or understanding (b) rather than a correct belief or understanding (c):

1. Eve's taking the forbidden fruit (Gen.3:6)

(a) disobeying God's command;

(b) taking the serpent's word over the Lord's, that the Lord was keeping some pleasure from her;

(c) the Lord knew what was best for her.

2. Adam's taking the forbidden fruit (Gen.3:6)

(a) being influence by his wife contrary to God's command;

(b) choosing to stay with his wife, after her sin, rather than with the Lord in the garden;

(c) his relationship with the Lord is the most important thing.

3. Moses' murder of the Egyptian (Ex.2:12)

(a) taking someone's life;

(b) taking injustice into his own hands for revenge;

(c) God would keep His promise to deliver His people in His own way and time.

4. Achan's theft of the Babylonian garment at Jericho (Josh.7:1)

(a) taking for himself what belonged to God;

(b) that it wouldn't matter to God if He didn't get all that was His;

(c) God expects us to give Him all that is His.

5. King Saul's sparing of Agag's life (1 Sam.15:8)

(a) disobedience, due to his fear of the people;

(b) destroying just most of the Amalekites would satisfy God;

(c) God expects to be obeyed totally.

6. Saul of Tarsus' persecution of the Christians (Acts 8:3; 1 Tim.1:13)

(a) imprisoning and executing the followers of Christ;

(b) he thought they were heretics to Judaism;

(c) Christ is Israel's Messiah.

7. Peter's denial of the Lord (Matt.26:72)

(a) he denied his association with Christ;

(b) he was afraid he would be arrested also;

(c) Christ had previously told Peter that He would be delivered up to death.

8. Ananias' & Saphira's theft of the proceeds of the sale of property (Acts 5:2)

(a) lying;

(b) contributing something and keeping part secretly will be OK;

(c) we need to keep commitments to the Lord and be honest.

Acting Responsibly

People sometimes need to be helped to see that they are responsible for their own actions (Ezek.18:20), that they do have the ability to respond in one way or another. It is all too easy to blame other people or blame our circumstances for the way things are and to feel helpless to change them. When they say, "I can't do that", it often really means that they won't. It will be difficult for them to make progress if they always see themselves as a victim, under the control of others. People do not always like to be accountable; it is often easier to blame someone else for problems. One of the things a counselor can do in a particular situation is show them what their options are and how to choose wisely.

Habitual Behaviour

People tend to do many things by habit. Some habits are good; some can be destructive. Habitual behaviour is based on the notion of "pay-offs" or rewards - the benefit we think we will get from it. We do things repeatedly because, consciously or unconsciously, we like what happens when we do them (or we prefer it to what we think the alternatives would be). Eliminating undesirable habits may require eliminating these payoffs. Many types of things can be payoffs, such as monetary rewards, the desire for approval, companionship, a sense of health and well-being, and a sense of achievement. Payoffs can even be negative, such as self-punishment (where the person feels guilty) or vindictiveness (where they are angry). Negative payoffs tend to support destructive behaviour, such as getting revenge.

Sometimes there may be a conflict between an immediate payoff (such as eating something tasty) and longer-term consequences (such as obesity or high cholesterol). In these cases, the shorter-term payoff usually wins out - it is the path of least resistance. A scriptural example of this is when Esau sold his birthright to get a meal (Gen.25:33). Overcoming conflict between short-term and long-term payoffs usually requires finding a way of making the longer-term payoff more visible at the time when the decision is being made (such as by placing a full-length mirror on the refrigerator door).

Emotions

All of us were originally made in the likeness of God, and so we have an emotional capacity. This enables us to be happy or sad, excited or glum, loving or hateful, and so on. Negative emotions however are the result of the sinful nature we all have, and they have at their root our self-centredness.

Feelings are not right or wrong in themselves; they are a reflection of how we interpret our circumstances, and so they serve as a symptom of our thinking. Telling someone not to feel a certain way is not helpful; they do feel that way because of what they believe to be true. For example, some people may regard certain news as good, while others regard the same news as not good. And so, just like our behaviour, our emotions are the result of our thinking and beliefs. As we saw with the two on the road to Emmaus, changing someone's feelings requires changing their understanding of reality - their thinking and beliefs.

Emotional states are communicated, either verbally or non-verbally, by various symptoms. These can include: silence, complaining, rebellion, over-eating, body language (e.g. rigidity, facial expression), and tone of voice. These symptoms enable others to recognize that we "seem upset". It is very hard for us to disguise this state of feeling.

Negative Emotions

Negative emotions can usefully be classified into five main groups, and scripture has much to say about them. Diagnosing the major negative emotion that someone is experiencing can be extremely useful in getting to understand their underlying problem. This emotional state can often take the form of a particular type of obstacle which is preventing them (or they perceived to be preventing them) from achieving their personal goals.

The five main groups of negative emotions are:

- Guilt - This arises when we violate our core personal values in the pursuit of a goal. The emotion of shame is similar, but it is related to violating other people's perceived values, and thus reducing their estimation of the person.

- Anxiety - This arises from a sense of being helpless in achieving personal goals, because of uncontrollable circumstances. It is a fear due to uncertainty.

- Anger - This arises from someone or something blocking the achievement of a personal goal.

- Low self-esteem - This arises from (usually) long-held) views of being incapable or unworthy of achieving personal goals.

- Depression - This arises from believing that achieving a personal goal is impossible and hopeless.

These feeling can vary widely in intensity, and can also occur in combinations. They are discussed in chapters 6 through 10.

6. UNDERSTANDING OUR DEADLY SINS

Lusts are our inner dispositions to sinful behaviour that we inherit as part of our sinful nature. They exist in everyone, in varying degrees. One categorization of these is what has been known for centuries as "the seven deadly sins". They are described as deadly because, if left unchecked, they will become ingrained (as "traits"), increasingly dominate our thinking, and thus lead to destructive behaviour. They are as follows:

Pride

> *"all that is in the world—the lust of the flesh, the lust of the eyes, and the pride of life - is not of the Father but is of the world"* (1 Jn.2:16).

Pride is having an unrealistically inflated self-concept. At a deeper level it is the conviction that I don't need God – the illusion of autonomy, of being in control of your own life. It was the original sin, by Lucifer. Pride is so serious that it calls forth resistance and opposition from God Himself (Jas.4:6). Pride ("no one can tell me what to do") denies the lordship of Christ, by refusing His authority and supremacy. It is an error in our thinking, our beliefs. Making ourselves pre-eminent is the core of the sin of pride.

> *"... you have said in your heart: 'I will ascend into heaven, I will exalt my throne ... I will be like the Most High"* (Is.14:13-14).

> *"God resists the proud, but gives grace to the humble"* (Jas.4:6; 1 Pet.5:5).

Manifestations of pride ("ego") include:

- wanting to take the credit;
- wanting to appear to be the expert;
- always having to be 'right';
- wanting control over others;
- craving attention;
- hungering for praise;
- rebelling against submission;
- not willing to apologize or admit error;
- refusing advice;
- being strongly opinionated and argumentative;
- being critical of others, while rejecting criticism of ourselves;
- faking humility;
- flaunting our rights and privileges;
- being inconsiderate;
- being over-sensitive; and
- being hypocritical.

The other six deadly sins are all based on pride, because they involve rebellion against God's law. It was Satan's first sin, and it gave rise to the others. Another case of overwhelming pride was Pharaoh, who "hardened his heart" against the Lord. His ambition to be right at all costs overwhelmed the facts and logic presented to him. He quarreled with Moses and was combative, and it destroyed him. Pride asserts that "MINE is the kingdom and the power and the glory". The model for us is Christ, who had every reason to be proud but was supremely humble (Phil.2:5-8).

> "Keep back Your servant also from presumptuous sins; Let them not have dominion over me. Then I shall be blameless, and I shall be innocent of great transgression" (Ps. 19:13).

"... let him who thinks he stands take heed lest he fall" (1 Cor.10:12).

"Why do you boast in evil, O mighty man? ...God shall likewise destroy you forever; ... the righteous also shall see and fear, and shall laugh at him, saying, Here is the man who did not make God his strength ..." (Ps.52:1-6).

"Let this mind be in you which was also in Christ Jesus, who, being in the form of God, did not consider it robbery to be equal with God, but made Himself of no reputation, taking the form of a bondservant, and coming in the likeness of men. And being found in appearance as a man, He humbled Himself and became obedient to the point of death, even the death of the cross" (Phil.2:5-8).

Pride is often described in the world as being a positive attribute (e.g. pride in accomplishment, pride in culture, "gay pride"), and certainly justifiable ("I have my pride, you know", which is really referring to proper self-esteem). Yet we know from scripture that pride is a serious cause of sin and is based on fundamentally wrong beliefs.

Envy

"... laying aside all malice, all guile, hypocrisy, envy, and all evil speaking ..." (1 Pet.2:1-2).

Envy is sorrow in the face of someone else's good. It is the desire for something or some trait belonging to that other person. (It is different from jealousy, in the scriptural sense of the word, which is the desire to keep what is your own. Jealousy is not always wrong; God is a jealous God (Ex.20:5), but He is never envious.) Envy was the motive of those who delivered Christ up to be killed (Matt.27:18). A scriptural example of envy is King Saul in his attitude to David (1 Sam.18:6-9).

Most sins offer pleasure or profit – for a while. Pride offers preeminence; anger promises revenge; greed offers wealth; sloth offers ease; lust offers sensation; and gluttony offers abundance. But envy is different; it offers nothing good. Envy comes from (a) comparing ourselves with other people, and (b) concluding that what they have is better. Comparing and concluding can become habits. It results in degrading our own things. The habit can only be cured by dealing with the underlying sinful lust of envy.

Envy often begins in our lives with sibling rivalry, which is common in many families. Children often think their parents treat them unfairly relative to their brothers and sisters, and this rivalry can continue into adulthood. Sibling rivalry, which is imagined unfairness or mistreatment, is actually envy. Envy uses other people as our standards of comparison, rather than objective standards. We can learn that we have been given the power to rejoice in God's good gifts to others, and to realize that the qualities and abilities came from God, and are therefore good and what we need, even if sometimes they seem to be obstacles or limitations.

Signs of envy include:

- complaining ("sour grapes");
- put downs;
- being critical (especially when someone is being praised); and
- exceptional competitiveness (enjoying beating someone just for the sake of it).

It results in a life with little peace or joy. It can result in us disliking someone without really knowing why. Envy can also be linked with pride and with low self-esteem. Envy is a sinful lust that comes from within. Love requires us to rejoice in another's good (1 Cor.13:6), not mourn over it. Love and envy are incompatible. Scripture warns us of the danger of comparing ourselves with each other. We are instructed about putting away envy.

"That which proceeds out of the man, that is what defiles the man. For from within, out of the heart of men, proceed the evil thoughts ... envy ..." (Mk.7:20-22 NASB).

"... they, measuring themselves by themselves, and comparing themselves among themselves, are not wise" (2 Cor.10:12).

"... laying aside all malice, all guile, hypocrisy, envy, and all evil speaking" (1 Pet.2:1).

"Let us not become conceited, provoking one another, envying one another" (Gal.5:26).

Anger (Wrongful)

"I desire therefore that the men pray everywhere, lifting up holy hands, without wrath and doubting" (1 Tim.2:8).

Sinful anger is defined as an inordinate desire for revenge, even if it is not carried out. The intent to hurt is malice (Eph.4:31). It includes peeved moments, nursed grudges, and irritated outbursts that we tend to self-justify. It can be moderate or violent rage. It can harden into bitterness (also Eph.4:31). Vindictive anger is a deadly sin. It can involve:

- harbouring resentment;
- thinking about getting even;
- arguing;
- quarreling;
- fighting;
- being sullen;
- being sarcastic;

- being cynical;
- being insulting;
- being critical;
- often getting indignant;
- desiring harm for others.

Anger is also a feeling (see previous chapter on feelings).

Greed

> "Neither the sexually immoral nor idolaters nor adulterers nor
> male prostitutes nor homosexual offenders nor thieves nor the
> greedy nor drunkards nor slanderers nor swindlers will inherit
> the kingdom of God" (1 Cor.6:9-10 NIV).

Greed is love of possessions. It is an inordinate or excessive desire to acquire in order to possess things, especially possessing more than we need. It is the opposite of moderation (temperance). With the materialistic influence of society all around us, it is hard to escape at least some degree of greed, even if it less than average. It's often hard to see our own greed. Greed is insidious in that we may be tempted to think that we'll be satisfied once we get what we want, whereas in fact our greed just grows; we keep wanting more. Research indicates that it gets worse with age. Scriptural examples of greed include Gehazi (2 Kin.5:20-27), Judas (Jn.12:4-6; Matt.26:14,15) and Ananias and Saphira (Acts 5:1-10).

> "... where your treasure is, there your heart will be also" (Luke
> 12:34).

> "You cannot serve God and mammon" (Matthew 6:24).

Greed is based on a belief that is a formula for failure: "the more things we get, the happier we will be." We are constantly brainwashed in this world about how contentment comes from procuring stuff. The Christian viewpoint is opposite. The New Testament has two words for greed. One means a reaching or grasping for something. The other means coveting. Coveting is being fixated on what belongs rightly to someone else.

> *"... joyfully accepted the plundering of your goods, knowing that you have a better and an enduring possession for yourselves in heaven"* (Heb.10:34).

> *"... the love of money is a root of all kinds of evil, for which some have strayed from the faith in their greediness, and pierced themselves through with many sorrows."* (1 Tim. 6:10).

> *"put to death your members which are on the earth: fornication, uncleanness, passion, evil desire, and covetousness, which is idolatry"* (Col.3:5).

> *"Take heed and beware of covetousness, for one's life does not consist in the abundance of the things he possesses."* (Lk.12:15-16).

It's no sin to have wealth. Many people in scripture were wealthy. Money is a stewardship for which we are responsible. The issue is what we do with it. Having more money than we need can lead to arrogance, showing off, a lax lifestyle, or a desire for entertainment or pleasure.

Symptoms of greed include:

- only doing things if there's some money in it for us;
- stinginess;
- slowness in paying debts;
- lack of generosity; and
- using questionable means to get or save money (e.g. tax

evasion).

Greed can be a real problem in a marriage. One spouse may be free spender, but the other a saver or a tight controller of money; they can become adversaries over money. Solving this requires taking the focus off each other's greed and on to their own. Loving and giving are incompatible with greed.

Sloth

> *"His lord answered and said unto him, 'Thou wicked and slothful servant'"* (Matt.25:26 KJV).

Sloth is excessive and irresponsible laziness. It can be linked with depression, and can sometimes have some physical causes. But sloth itself is a sinful lust. It often causes us to say, "I can't ..." (despite Philippians 4:13: "I can do all things through Christ who strengthens me.") Inactivity is a choice.

Symptoms include:

- a faint spirit;
- heaviness (Is.61:3);
- lack of desire to accomplish anything;
- dejection;
- listlessness;
- aversion to effort;
- the feeling that effort is useless;
- being weak-willed;
- not attempting to break bad habits;
- constantly seeking bodily ease and comfort;
- engaging often in trivial activities;
- preferring idleness;
- drifting along in mediocrity; and

- self-devaluation.

It can involve a feeling of alienation from God, and a sense of no will power.

"The slothful man roasteth not that which he took in hunting" (Prov.12:27).

"Not slothful [lacking in diligence or zeal] in business" (Rom.12:11).

Sexual Lust

> *"the Lord knows how to deliver the godly out of temptations and to reserve the unjust under punishment for the day of judgment, and especially those who walk according to the flesh in the lust of uncleanness"* (2 Pet.2:9-10).

Sexual lust is intense sexual craving. Sex is a God-given good, in the right situation. Its purpose is intimacy, not selfish gratification. The world's view is that, as long as sex is consensual, it is not immoral or harmful. They think that it must be good because it's pleasurable. The media and entertainment industry can be very persuasive, and they emphasize the pleasurable aspect, not the downside. Hedonism (the love of pleasure) is "in" these days. Lust is a slippery slope. Society's standards, as led by the entertainment industry, are becoming increasingly permissive. Illicit practices move quickly from the unthinkable to the thinkable to interesting to acceptable to codification into law. This has the effect of "systematic desensitization" – we become numbed by repetition. But the Bible's moral truth is not a burden, it's a gift designed for our well-being.

The Bible condemns more than the act of illicit sex; it condemns even fantasizing about it (Matt.5:27,28). Most sins begin in the mind, but perhaps none more powerfully or pleasurably than lust. Just thinking about it can cause arousal. And fantasizing often leads to overt behaviour. The Bible teaches chastity (not celibacy). Sexual lust can become an addiction, especially with men. It can also cause problems of depression, guilt and anxiety. There is correlation with people who exhibit tendencies to rebellion and also withdrawal to a fantasy world.

"Those who walk according to the flesh in the lust of uncleanness and despise authority. They are presumptuous, self-willed" (2 Pet.2:10).

Overcoming lust requires removing ourselves from the source of temptation.

"For this is the will of God, your sanctification: that you should abstain from sexual immorality; that each of you should know how to possess his own vessel in sanctification and honor, not in passion of lust, like the Gentiles who do not know God." (1 Thess.4:3-6).

Gluttony

"the enemies of the cross of Christ: whose end is destruction, whose god is their belly" (Phil.3:18-19).

Gluttony (like sexual lust) is overindulging in pursuit of worldly pleasure, eating too much (or too fast), being preoccupied with food, drinking alcohol too much or too often, or being overly engaged in the enjoyment of them. They are both perversions of God-given pleasures. They both make us susceptible to spiritual attack, as our animal natures war against the Spirit. Self-control is part of the fruit of the Spirit (Gal.5:23), and it needs to be cultivated. Gluttony is a triumph of our natural impulses over our wills. Even good things can become the object of gluttony. Gluttony can be in relation to food, TV, sports, etc.

While pleasure is of course attractive to us, excessive desire for it has very adverse effects, such as boredom – we run out of material. Christ was falsely accused of being a glutton (Matt.11:16-19). It can result in duties and service to God and other people being neglected. Hedonism is the natural state of sinful humankind. It cares only about feeling good.

Some people have a constant dread of boredom, and they do everything possible to avoid it, always seeking novel circumstances and fresh entertainment. Satisfying these desires doesn't eliminate the boredom; it just creates a greater desire for more. There is no permanent "joy" (source of satisfaction). We generally do not like being at total rest, with no goals or passions, without occupation or diversion or effort. We like to keep busy, doing something. Boredom makes us feel our loneliness, inadequacy, purposelessness, dependence, helplessness and emptiness. It is a spiritual disorder. It is manifest in lack of an overarching purpose in life ("a reason for getting out of bed in the morning"). Our overarching purpose is in effect the god we serve. Christ's wisdom on the subject was (paradoxically) that, if God's kingdom and righteousness became our overarching goal, we'd not only get that but also all the other things we need. Boredom can be an indicator that we have (perhaps inadvertently) chosen to live for pleasure. It can be an alarm that we are serving the wrong god.

"Seek first the kingdom of God and His righteousness, and all these things shall be added to you" (Matt.6:33).

The law of God to Israel had severe consequences for a glutton and a drunkard, and related them to stubbornness and rebellion (Deut.21:18-21). Paul said that he disciplined his body and brought it into subjection, so that his work for God wouldn't be nullified (1 Cor.9:27).

"... the drunkard and the glutton will come to poverty" (Prov.23:21).

7. DEALING WITH GUILT AND SHAME

"Godly sorrow produces repentance leading to salvation, not to be regretted; but the sorrow of the world produces death" (2 Cor.7:10).

Feelings of guilt result from believing that we have violated one of our core values in the pursuit of a goal, and may have realised we have indulged in one or other of the fleshly lusts we were looking at in the previous chapter. It results in inner conflict. Shame, on the other hand, is the feeling we experience when we believe we have violated others' expectations of us. Guilt is a God-given faculty, to alert us to wrong-doing in our lives and so correct it. As the verse above states, godly sorrow is intended to be remedial, not destructive. Our core values may or may not be properly based on our God-given conscience, but that conscience can become distorted through misuse.

The Case of Adam and Eve

We don't have to go very far in the Bible to come across people with guilt feelings. In Genesis 3, Adam and Eve had just disobeyed God's command about the forbidden fruit, and instantly they experienced feelings they'd never had before - feelings that come with being a sinner.

Firstly, it says that they became afraid - afraid of being rejected. They'd never been afraid before, and fear is a very strong motivator. In fact the Bible says that only love is stronger than fear (1 Jn.4:18). And so feeling guilty can make us afraid. Secondly, they were ashamed - it affected their relationship with each other. Thirdly, they tried a cover-up - with leaves. But it didn't work; it never does. Cover-ups only make things worse, and they take a lot of energy. Fourthly, they hid. Before this they'd been out in the open; now they withdrew - they didn't want the Lord God to see them. They felt alienated for the first time ever.

And fifthly, they began to blame each other. Passing the blame is a fine art these days, but it started away back in the garden of Eden.

Previously Adam had seen that Eve was God's perfect provision for him, just what he needed. Now she became someone to blame, and there was even an implied blaming of God: *"the woman you gave me"*. And in turn Eve turned and blamed the serpent. Fear, shame, cover-up, alienation, passing the blame - all part of this emotion of feeling guilty.

Some people live their whole lives plagued by guilt, because it never goes away on its own. It can kill our Christian lives and vitality, and yet it's totally avoidable. Because the guilt for all our wrong-doings was borne away by Christ on Calvary.

Why Do We Feel Guilty?

Inside, when we feel guilty, we have inner turmoil - it feels as though two parts of us are in conflict (which they are). What has happened is that we have violated one of our own personal values. For example, I might truly believe that I'm an honest person. But if I lie to someone, I will feel guilty. I may say: "I'm a moral person", but if I yield to sexual temptation I will feel guilty.

Everyone has these values; they're part of our upbringing and our culture. We tend to start out adopting our parents' values, then we become exposed to a wider set of influences - such as teachers, our peers, and society at large. By the time we reach maturity, we have established our own values. They are our personal standards, and when we think we've violated them, we feel uncomfortable - whether they are consistent with God's values or not.

Shame

Shame is somewhat different. Shame relates to our relationship with other people. We feel ashamed when we think we've violated their expectations of us, and so lost their respect. When we violate God's standards, we should feel our guilt towards God, but sometimes we feel more ashamed towards other people than towards God. Which is perhaps an indication that our priorities are somewhat distorted.

How Is Your Conscience?

One of the results of Adam and Eve's sin was that they were given a conscience - the inner knowledge of good and evil. And they've passed it down to all of us. C.S. Lewis said that this inner conscience is one of the greatest proofs that mankind was created by God, and it led him to salvation in Christ. He said, "All human beings have an in-built notion that they ought to behave a certain way, and they can't get rid of it; yet they don't in fact behave that way most of the time." He said that observing our behaviour from outside would not reveal this, but we as humans know within ourselves that there is this force (which we often don't follow) that tells us whether something is right or wrong.

The Bible tells us that our consciences can be strong or weak. They can also be good or evil, depending on how we've responded to them in the past. It's like a red and green traffic light in our heads, given by God, telling us to go ahead or not. The Bible says it *"accuses or excuses"* (Rom.2:15).

Our conscience is like a muscle. If we use it and act on it, it will become stronger and stronger. If we repeatedly ignore it, it will eventually stop talking to us altogether. Someone has said: the first time, your conscience shouts, "Don't do it"; the next time it says, "Don't do it"; the next time it whispers, "Don't do it"; and the next time - nothing. The Bible refers to this as it being *"seared with a hot iron"* (1 Tim.4:2).

The apostle Paul said, "*I myself always strive to have a conscience without offense toward God and men.*" In other words, he didn't want to feel guilty. How healthy is your conscience (Acts 24:16)?

Are All Feelings of Guilt Bad?

Why did God give us the capacity to feel guilty, to know when we've acted against our conscience? Was it just to make us feel badly, or was there a positive purpose to it? Feeling guilty when we sin is a sure sign that God is trying to get our attention. It's when He stops doing that that we're in real trouble. He doesn't want our sin to destroy us. A defining characteristic of a follower of Jesus Christ, and of a church of God, is how seriously it treats sin. We can get outraged at other people's sin, but when was the last time we were outraged about our own sin?

We are given this sense of guilt so that, when we are in fact guilty, we will take the proper steps to get rid of our guilt. Those guilt feelings are referred to as *"godly sorrow"* (2 Cor.7:10) and their purpose is always to restore us. It is contrasted with the world's sorrow, which is inherently destructive. Psychologists regard guilt feelings as a mental problem; however, God describes them as a moral problem. Psychologists can suggest how we can try to overcome our guilt feelings, but with God repentance is always a necessary step. If we are guilty of some sin, it is futile to try to bury it, or cover it up or ignore it. We just drive it deeper within ourselves, and it will eat away at us - physically, mentally and spiritually.

Both Peter and Judas committed serious sins against the Lord. One denied Him and the other betrayed Him. Was one worse than the other? Or was the difference how they reacted afterwards? Why did Peter get back up, but Judas committed suicide? Christ prayed for Peter, and he found repentance; Judas did not.

How Do We Stop Feeling Guilty?

The first thing we have to do to eliminate feelings of guilt is to determine whether or not we really are guilty - not by society's norms, or other peoples' opinions, but by God's Word. When the Bible refers to guilt, it's always talking about breaking God's law. All sin is against God (Ps.51:4), which is why God can forgive all sin. The Bible never tells us to try to motivate people by trying to make them feel guilty - giving them a "guilt trip". Guilt feelings are only good for motivating correction of sin. It is the work of the Holy Spirit to convict us that we've sinned (Jn.16:8). Because if we really are guilty, there is no remedy except repentance. And if we're not guilty, then repentance isn't the answer. What we want is for our conscience to be so in line with God's Word that it's giving us the right signals. That means we have to know what the Bible teaches, and we have to believe it - be convinced about it.

Repentance

Repentance is much more than just saying "I'm sorry, please forgive me". In fact it's not something we can do all by ourselves; it's something than God grants (or withholds) (see 2 Tim.2:25). And it's much more than just not liking the consequences of our sin. For example, when Esau surrendered his birthright to Jacob, he was in tears about it. But he never obtained repentance from God - a true change of heart (Heb.12:17). He just didn't like the fact that he wasn't going to get the double inheritance of the firstborn. What gets in the way of our repentance for sin is shifting the blame, minimizing the offense and rationalizing our actions (all of which we tend naturally to be good at).

Genuine repentance usually involves six things, depending on the circumstances:

1. confessing the sin, and acknowledging the facts - as opposed to denial or avoidance; we can tend to resist this acknowledgement because of pride;
2. stopping the sin - permanently (and getting help if it's an addiction);
3. admitting to God how sinful it is, which first involves

acknowledging it to yourself -which can be very hard;
4. admitting it, and the damage it has done, to others affected by it, if any;
5. making full amends, to the extent possible; and
6. accepting the consequences of our actions.

Sometimes there are lasting consequences of our wrong-doing, even after we've genuinely repented, and we have to be prepared to accept these. Galatians 6:7 says that *"God is not mocked; for whatever a man sows, that he will also reap"*. We are forgiven, but we're not protected from the consequences of our sin.

Within a church of God, overseers together sometimes have the difficult task of discerning true repentance in order to commend a person for restoration to the assembly or to service within it. These same things are what they look for.

God's Forgiveness and Cleansing

When we confess our sin to God, we are assured of His complete forgiveness and cleansing: *"If we confess our sins, He is faithful and just to forgive us our sins and to cleanse us from all unrighteousness"* (1 Jn.1:9). Notice that this is based totally on God's faithfulness and God's righteousness; it's got nothing to do with whether or not we deserve it. He will always forgive when we genuinely repent, because Christ took our guilt away on Calvary. No sin is beyond this. What this forgiveness does is to restore our relationship with God - put us back on good terms with Him. He can now bless us instead of having to discipline us for our correction.

Unconfessed sin is a great barrier to our personal spiritual growth and also to the progress of a church of God. It brings everything to a halt. For example, when Achan sinned when Israel defeated Jericho, Israel was stymied until Joshua uncovered it and dealt with it. It was one man's secret sin and yet God said, "Israel has sinned". Sin must be dealt with. Repentance is a key survival skill of a genuine Christian.

God is able to forget our sins when He forgives them. However other people may not forgive us when we confess to them, and they may have long memories. We have to leave that with God. That is their problem. Our responsibility is to truly acknowledge what we have done, and its seriousness, and do all we can to make amends. It only takes one person to confess, but it takes both to reconcile, and so reconciliation with others is not always assured.

Feeling Guilty When We're Not

Feeling guilty when we're not in fact guilty is a big problem, because repentance isn't the answer. What is the answer? How do we get rid of the negative feeling? Here is where real faith in the Word of God comes in to triumph over those false emotions. Let's look at three distinct situations.

We Were Previously Guilty but Have Been Forgiven

It's quite possible to apply 1 John 1:9 and yet not 'feel' like we are forgiven. This is because we are relying on our emotions to tell us what's true, when God's Word tells us differently. We have to take God at His word even when it doesn't feel like it. For example, Joseph told his brothers he had forgiven them, but they didn't really believe it and they were afraid he would take revenge on them once their father died.

And so what's the remedy? Keep reading and meditating on that scripture, asking God to drive the truth of it deep into your soul until you are convinced it really is true. When you truly believe that, because you sincerely confessed your sin to God, He has fully forgiven and cleansed you, then the feeling will go away. Your growing faith in God's Word is what will triumph over those feelings.

In Psalm 32 David describes how his guilt made him feel, and then how differently he felt after he had openly and honestly laid it before the Lord: *"When I kept silent, my bones grew old. Through my groaning all the day long. For day and night Your hand was heavy upon me; My vitality was turned into the drought of summer"* (v.3,4).

He felt lethargic and depressed, and he couldn't get it out of his mind. Guilt feelings made him miserable. They were clearly very destructive. Then he said:

> *"I acknowledged my sin to You, and my iniquity I have not hidden. I said, "I will confess my transgressions to the LORD," and You forgave the iniquity of my sin."* ... *"Blessed is he whose transgression is forgiven, whose sin is covered. Blessed is the man to whom the LORD does not impute iniquity, and in whose spirit there is no deceit"* (vv.5, 1,2).

What a difference.

It Wasn't Wrong

A second possibility is that what we did wasn't actually wrong at all. It's a great relief when we realize this, and that those debilitating feelings are groundless. In 1 Corinthians 8, the apostle Paul said that he had liberty to do certain things that other Christians thought were wrong. He limited himself to make sure that he didn't stumble them (because that itself would be wrong) but he said the problem was that they had a "weak" conscience. That is, it was poorly informed. Their conscience may have been based on assumptions or on traditions, but it wasn't firmly based on the Word of God. It wasn't that these Christians thought it was OK to do things that were wrong, but just the opposite. They thought it was wrong to do things that were actually OK. They felt guilty when they weren't guilty, which is very unproductive.

What's the remedy this time? It's the same thing. Let the Word of God so convince us that it determines our conscience. Again it's faith over feelings. My feelings of false guilt will only disappear when I truly believe what the Word of God teaches, even when it differs from what I've always thought. I'll stop feeling guilty for things that aren't wrong. Otherwise I'll be trapped in guilt feelings with no way out.

We Aren't the Ones Responsible

A third reason for wrongly feeling guilty is by taking on ourselves responsibility for what other people have done - even though we can't control that. Parents often feel responsible for how their children behave in public, even though they are doing everything they can do as parents. Conversely children invariably feel at fault when their parents are having marital troubles, and they will often do almost anything to bring them back together.

People who have suffered abuse as children typically feel guilty - that somehow it was their fault, and they may have great trouble getting over the effects of this until they realize the truth is that they were victims, and not responsible at all for what was done to them. A biblical example of this is Tamar in 2 Samuel 13, when she was raped by Amnon; note her reaction in verses 19-20: "*Then Tamar put ashes on her head, and tore her robe of many colors that was on her, and laid her hand on her head and went away crying bitterly ... So Tamar remained desolate in her brother Absalom's house.*" She thought she was guilty.

Overseers can sometimes engage in self-flagellation about wayward saints as though it was the overseers' fault, when in fact they have provided all the care they could. We are not accountable for other peoples' actions, just for how we interact with them. Scripture teaches us this important point - that we are only accountable for our own actions (including how we act towards other people). Ezekiel 18:19,20 says:

*"You say, 'Why should the son not bear the guilt of the father?'
Because the son has done what is lawful and right, and has
kept all My statutes and done them, he shall surely live. The
soul who sins shall die. The son shall not bear the guilt of the father, nor the father bear the guilt of the son. The righteousness
of the righteous shall be upon himself, and the wickedness of the
wicked shall be upon himself."*

Each of us is only responsible for our self, and that is a full-time job.
Only when we are truly convinced of this scriptural truth will our guilt
feelings go away when it's someone else who has done wrong and it was
outside our control.

Overcoming Feelings of Guilt

Some people are crippled by guilt feelings for many years. Those feelings don't go away on their own. And they can severely hamper our
Christian life, as well as our physical health and our relationships with
others. None of us can avoid making mistakes in life; James said so: *"We
all stumble in many things"* (Jas.3:2). But Christ, by His sacrifice, has
made recovery always possible, no matter what the sin was.

Success in life isn't measured by what we attain, but by what we overcome. Don't let guilt feelings from real or imagined sins in your past
hold you captive. God doesn't mean you to live that way. The remedy
for true guilt is repentance and confession. And the remedy for false
guilt is inner conviction in the truth and reality of the Word of God as
it applies to that situation. Christ died so that we wouldn't have to live
with feelings of guilt.

8. DEALING WITH ANGER AND FRUSTRATION

"the wrath of man does not produce the righteousness of God" (Jas.1:20).

It has been said that you can tell a lot of things about a person by what makes them angry. What sort of things make you angry? Sometimes it may just be little things, and you may wonder why you reacted so strongly. You may realize that you were reading a lot into the situation that really wasn't there. We can often regard peoples' innocent actions as intentional slights.

The anger "family" of emotions ranges from mild irritation to outright rage. It includes bitterness, frustration, momentary flare-ups and also life-long grudges. It's possible to stay angry for years. For example, one man who left a church thirty years ago is still mad at how people treated him at the time - even though most of them are now dead. He is still angry at people who are in the grave. That's a long time to stay mad. He's never gotten over it.

It's even possible to be angry at God. Perhaps is associated with grief at losing a loved one, which God could have prevented. It can also last a long time. It even happened in the Bible; Jesus said to the Jews *"Are you angry with me because I healed a man on the Sabbath?"* (Jn.7:23).

Blow-up or Clam-up?

People react to triggers differently. Some people blow up; others clam up. Blowing up is one way of expressing anger; clamming up is repressing it. We either explode or we implode, but neither one is healthy. Expressing our anger outwardly can be done physically or verbally. Physical responses (such as hitting someone, pounding our fist, or stamping our feet) are usually trained out of us after childhood, and so more frequently our anger comes out in what we say - attacking the person verbally. The old saying *"sticks and stones may break my bones, but words can never hurt me"* is not true; words can hurt a lot. Certainly neither of these things is the Christian way to deal with anger.

On the other hand, repressing our anger doesn't make it dissipate; it just internalizes it, where it can do us a lot of damage. We may become silent and withdrawn, like the prodigal son's older brother who wouldn't even come into the house when his brother came home. Repressing our anger can lead to "passive-aggressive" behaviour, where we appear to be passive but are actually being manipulative, such as refusing to co-operate. Hebrews 12:15 talks about *"the root of bitterness"* - a bitterness that grows up within us when we've been hurt in some way. It becomes a deep grudge. And it destroys, not the person who caused the hurt (they may not even be aware of it), but the person who stays bitter.

The context of Hebrews 12:15 is Esau, who despised his birthright and gave it away to his brother Jacob. When he realized that he'd been taken advantage of, he was really angry. Later Jacob also stole the firstborn's blessing from him, and he had to run away to get away from his brother. But Esau was also angry at his father for letting all this happen and, to spite him, he married an Ishmaelite woman against his father's wishes. Anger can cause us to act out of spite, just to hurt someone, even if it doesn't do us any good either.

We don't make good decisions that way. Esau wanted revenge, and it ate away at him for years. Ephesians 4:26 says: *"Don't let the sun go down on your wrath"*. In other words, don't go to bed mad. That's gives us an absolute maximum of 24 hours to stay angry. How many suns went down on Esau's wrath? And it cost him dearly - alienation from his father and brother for many years.

Getting Revenge

Anger often results in us wanting revenge, out of an imagined sense of justice. We want to hurt the person who hurt us just as they've hurt us, whether it was intentional or not. That's a natural instinct. Society tells us "Don't get mad, get even". But revenge is not an option for the Christian. God has reserved that for Himself. *"Vengeance is mine; I will repay", says the Lord"* (Heb.10:30). That's why Christ never fought back. Instead He committed Himself to Him who judges righteously (1 Pet.2:23). He knew God would deal properly with all injustice.

Anger Literally Kills

Someone has said "The man who can make me angry can kill me". And it's true. There are many effects of being angry. Anger can be a very strong emotion and cause us to lose control of ourselves. We literally do become "mad" - somewhat irrational. Physically the blood flows from our brain to our extremities, and so we become a bit stupid. For example, Cain was so angry at his sacrifice being rejected by God that he took it out on Abel by killing him; He committed murder. We may think we are at our strongest when we are angry, because we feel so aggressive, but we are actually weaker. It's good to remember that fact when we're getting angry at someone, such as a supplier who's giving us poor customer service.

Anger is very physically unhealthy for us. It can cause heart attacks and strokes. It is virtually impossible to hide the fact when we're angry. If we observe other people, we can always tell - for example, when they're stuck in traffic, or in a long lineup, or on the phone. Apparently there are fourteen different biological effects on our bodies when we get angry (such as faster breathing, a flow of adrenaline, increased blood pressure, and increased heart rate). We may get red in the face; our neck may stiffen; we may get rigid. We can't hide it. Other people can tell - and they will react to it, either by becoming hostile or becoming defensive.

From an inter-personal point of view, anger can seriously impair relationships and make people on edge around us - "walking on egg shells". We don't relate well with angry people. Proverbs 15:18 says, "*A wrathful man stirs up strife.*" Proverbs 22:24,25 says, "*Make no friendship with an angry man, and with a furious man do not go, lest you learn his ways*". Often we tend to take out our frustrations on those who are closest to us. It may not make sense, except that we feel safest in those relationships.

Spiritually, anger can be disastrous also. James 1:20 says, "*The wrath of man does not produce the righteousness of God.*" We're not doing God's work when we're angry or frustrated or bitter. 1 Timothy 2:8 says that it impedes our prayers: "*I desire therefore that the men pray everywhere, lifting up holy hands, without wrath and doubting*". And Ephesians 4:27 says that staying angry gives the devil an opening, and clearly that's not something that we want. This is not how God intends us to live.

What Causes Anger?

What's going on inside us when we feel anger rising up within us? Again, like the emotions of guilt and anxiety, it's a negative emotion that's related to us having our goals blocked. When that blockage is caused by an action of a person or a circumstance that occurs, anger is the emotion we feel. And, even when it is in fact a circumstance, we tend to personalize it. (For example, if my computer doesn't work, I can get mad at the engineers who developed the software, even though that might be totally unreasonable.) We tend to look for someone to blame. And so our anger is usually directed at people. We feel hurt and wounded. In fact when someone says (or shows) they are angry, substitute the word "hurt" and it will usually help to understand how they feel.

Is Anger Always Wrong?

Not all anger is wrong. It depends on the motivation. Matthew 5:22 refers to the wrong of being angry *"without a cause"*. But God Himself gets angry, and that's never wrong. Psalm 7:11 says *"God is angry with the wicked every day."* What makes God angry is when things that are His (they're called "holy") are treated as common-place - as though they were no different from other things. The worst sin that Israel was guilty of (among many) was idolatry - giving the worship that belonged to God to things that weren't gods at all. Worship is God's unique entitlement. He is a jealous God - but He is not an envious God. There is a difference in how scripture uses these words. Envy is what prompted the Jews to kill Jesus; they wanted what was His. But jealousy is wanting to keep what is rightfully ours. And it's even possible for us to be jealous for God - we call it "righteous indignation".

Jesus had righteous indignation in John 2:13-17 when He drove the money-changers out of the temple grounds. They were gouging people who had traveled long distances and needed to buy animals for the ceremonial sacrifices. Jesus said, *"Don't make my Father's house a house of merchandise".* He was angry, but not for Himself. He never got angry at how He Himself was treated. 1 Peter 2:23 says, *"when He was reviled, did not revile in return; when He suffered, He did not threaten, but committed Himself to Him who judges righteously".* He handed the revenge issue over to God. However, in our case, most of the things that make us angry are things that affect us personally.

The New Testament uses two different Greek words for this emotion. One is translated "anger" (the Greek is 'orge' and means a slow burn), and the other is translated "wrath" (the Greek is 'thumos' and means to flare up). We are taught about both. Ephesians 4:31 has them both in one verse: *"Let all wrath* [thumos] *and anger* [orge] *be put away from you"*.

How Can a Christian Combat Feelings of Anger?

Do we recognize sin?

Firstly, Ephesians 4:26 says, *"Be angry and sin not"*. Do we view our habitual tendencies to feel negatively towards others if things don't go as we want them as being sin, which therefore needs prompt acknowledgement and confession? Would we wish to react differently? Anger is something we have to make a choice about. If we are frequently frustrated or annoyed that others put roadblocks in the way of us achieving what we want, perhaps it's our expectations that need to change. If others don't obey our expectations or "rules" for them, is that a source of frustration since we can't enforce those rules?

Anyone who angers us controls us to a certain extent. They can determine how we feel and perhaps how we act. But we need to stay in control of ourselves. Proverbs 16:32 says *"He who is slow to anger is better than the mighty, and he who rules his spirit than he who takes a city"*. No one can make us mad without our consent. We need to be in control of our own spirits, and not allow anger to cause us to sin and become unhealthy.

Check the Assumptions

Secondly, James 1:19 tells us, *"Be swift to hear, slow to speak, slow to wrath"*. It tells us that because instinctively we do the opposite. "Swift to hear" - how often do we react angrily to something only to find out that we made a wrong assumption? The person didn't actually do what we thought they did or say what we thought they said. Or we may have assumed that what they did was deliberate - that they were just trying to make things difficult for us. It's amazing how our minds work that way - causing us to jump to conclusions. "Swift to hear" means listen carefully and check your assumptions, so that you won't regret it later. As one author puts it: "Seek first to understand before you seek to be understood". We often act instinctively, but a spiritual person learns to be deliberate and conscious in their actions.

"Slow to speak" is like "first counting to ten". Since we most often react in anger verbally rather than physically, it means to control our tongue (which is hard to do - James devotes a chapter to it in his epistle). Instead of saying accusingly "you did this" or "you said this", try saying "I feel this way about what you did (or said)". It puts it in terms of your own feelings and tends to make the person less defensive. It focuses instead on how the action affected you, which is what it's really about.

Forgive Them

Thirdly, Ephesians 4:32 says, *"forgiving one another, just as God in Christ forgave you."* If someone has hurt us, it is imperative that we forgive them. We are commanded to do this, and the great example is God who, unlike us, never ever needed to be forgiven Himself for anything. No matter what someone has done to us, we can be sure that God has forgiven us more than that in Christ.

Understanding Forgiveness

Forgiveness is not based on our feelings ("I don't feel like forgiving them"), it is a choice we make. Saying "I can't forgive them" really means "I won't forgive them". Forgiveness is giving up our right to revenge. It releases all those natural instincts that take offence, and turns them all over to God, who judges rightly. Forgiving someone brings freedom; in effect it releases us from being their prisoner. It can be difficult to do, but Jesus told one man to forgive seventy times seven times - in other words, until it became a habit. In effect, forgiveness is a gift we give ourselves.

When we forgive a person, we shouldn't stop there. We should also seek to be reconciled to them, which requires their active consent also. Hopefully being forgiven will cause a change in their wrong behaviour to enable reconciliation to take place (Jn.8:11), but we can't let that dictate our behaviour towards them. Being forgiven is not a license for them to behave badly and continue in sin; but that is not within our control. However, reconciliation should continue be the goal. Forgiveness just requires one person, but reconciliation requires both.

Overcoming Angry Feelings

Christians should not be angry people; not that we have any less provocation than other people, but we have been given extra resources to overcome it. God often uses people who irritate us as a refining process to remove a character flaw. He often uses these struggles to develop our character - somewhat like resistance weight training. *Tribulation produces perseverance; and perseverance, character; and character, hope"* (Rom.5:3). God is far more interested in our character than our comfort. He doesn't put us in the fire just to torment us, but to refine us. He keeps doing this until He sees the image of Christ being reflected in us. It's intended to make us better, not bitter, as the following poem by Arthur Ingler expresses:

He sat by a fire of seven-fold heat,

As He watched the precious ore;

And closer He bent with a searching gaze

As He heated it more and more;

He knew He had ore that could stand the test,

And He wanted the finest gold

To mould as a crown for the King to wear,

Set with gems of price untold.

So He laid our gold in the burning fire,

Though we'd surely have said to Him "no";

And He watched the dross that we had not seen;

As it melted, He saw it go.

And the gold grew brighter and yet more bright,

But our eyes were so dim with tears;

We saw just the fire, not the Master's hand,

And questioned with anxious fears.

Yet our gold shone out with a richer glow,

As it mirrored a form above,

That bent o'er the fire, though unseen by us,

With a look of ineffable love.

Can we think that it pleases His loving heart

To cause us a moment's pain?

Oh no, but He saw through the present cross

The bliss of eternal gain.

So He waited there with a watchful eye,

With a love that is strong and sure.

And His gold did not suffer a bit more heat

Than was needed to make it pure.

9. DEALING WITH ANXIETY AND FEAR

"The Lord is my helper; I will not fear" (Heb.13:6).

Are you a worrier - not just occasionally, but chronically? Do you often get uptight and stressed? If you answered 'yes', then are you also a control-oriented person, someone who likes to have everything under their control? Because the two often go together. In 2 Corinthians 7:5 the apostle Paul said, *"Outside are conflicts; inside are fears"*. We live in a world with many "stressors" - financial concerns, job insecurity, concerns about safety, raising our children in a world that is less Christian every day. We live in a stressful environment. Outside are conflicts; inside are fears. It all adds up to a lifestyle of stress, and too much stress brings distress, which is very unhealthy. Worrying can become a habit - a bad habit.

The Effects of Anxiety

What does too much worry and anxiety do to us? Mentally it tends to preoccupy us and consume our thoughts. It paralyses our minds so that we may have trouble concentrating on anything else. It may prevent us from sleeping and relaxing and acting productively. Being with an anxious person tends to make us a bit anxious - it's contagious. Physically, worry actually ages us. Symptoms include skin rashes, upset stomachs ("butterflies"), headaches, and the urge to urinate. It can attack our immune system, making us more susceptible to illness. It raises our blood pressure. There is a direct link between fear and heart attacks, such as Nabal experienced in 1 Samuel 25, and with *"men's hearts failing them from fear" in* Luke 21:26. Anxiety disorders are the most common form of mental illness today.

Worrying is an unproductive activity; it never solves problems - which is why there are so many references in scripture to "fear not" (63 in all). It can't change the past, but it can ruin the present. Spiritually, anxiety can stifle the work of God in us. In Matthew chapter 13, Jesus told the parable of the sower to illustrate how the Word of God works. Some of the seed, which is the Word of God, fell among thorns which (He said) represent *"the cares of this life"*, the things we care about, that matter to us. Anxiety is being too attached to what we care about, and the possible loss of it. The thorns choke the fruit that's growing from the implanted Word.

Fear is a very powerful motivator, but it's not a positive one - because it just motivates us to do anything to avoid the threat. It's a motivation away from the threat, but not to anything positive in particular. Fear of the unknown is just as powerful of fear of something we know about, because the body can't distinguish between real and imagined threats. Mark Twain once said, "I have been through some terrible things in my life, some of which actually happened".

Particularly powerful fears are:

- the fear of rejection;
- the fear of the unknown (which is why some people turn to horoscopes, fortune tellers, etc.);
- the fear of death;
- the fear of others' opinions (Prov.29:25 says that it's a snare);
- the fear of failure (resulting in refusal to try);
- the fear of betrayal (e.g. divorce, child abuse, gossip); and
- the fear of lack of things we need.

What's Going on Inside?

Job's friend Zophar said to him, *"My anxious thoughts make me answer, because of the turmoil within me"* (Job 20:2). Anxiety is the inner turmoil we have when a particular goal is important to us, but we feel help-less to achieve it It's not within our control. We are at the mercy of oth-ers or of outside circumstances. And so we worry about it. We feel the turmoil in the pit of our stomachs, and it's unhealthy. Sometimes it's just little things that do it.

What's the Remedy?

Telling someone not to worry isn't particularly helpful. (How often have you told someone not to worry and they said 'OK; I won't" and they stopped?) Yet the Bible tells us exactly that: "Do not worry". But it goes on to tell us how to do it.

The Case of Martha

Consider the case of Martha of Bethany, when the Lord came in one day with a number of His disciples.

> *"But Martha was distracted with much serving, and she ap-proached Him and said, "Lord, do You not care that my sister has left me to serve alone? Therefore tell her to help me." And Je-sus answered and said to her, "Martha, Martha, you are wor-ried and troubled about many things. But one thing is needed, and Mary has chosen that good part, which will not be taken away from her."* Why was she so distracted? This was a big occasion for her. She had to feed them and look after them, and Mary wasn't helping" (Lk.10:38-42).

Both Mary and Martha made a choice that day. Mary chose to take advantage of this unique opportunity to listen to the Lord speaking. Martha chose to be busy with work she thought needed doing - and she was anxious and troubled about many things. The things were le-gitimate, but they were the cares of this life, that choke and stifle. These people need to be fed, she may have thought, and what kind of a hostess would I be if I didn't put on a meal for them? But only one thing was needed, Christ said, and Mary had chosen it. Martha's anxiety was because of the choice she had made as to what was most important at that moment.

In Matthew 6:31-34 the Lord told His disciples not to worry about the necessities of life. That's what unbelievers do. But the disciples had a heavenly Father, He said, who had promised to take care of those things. Instead they were seek His kingdom and His righteousness, and all the other things needed would be provided. It was a matter of choice. Here again, faith in what God has said is the key to overcoming negative, unhealthy feelings. We need to look after God's things and trust Him to look after our things.

In the Upper Room

A second example is when the disciples were in the upper room on the night before Calvary. The Lord had said to them *"let not your hearts be troubled"* (Jn.4:1), because that's how they were feeling - anxious and troubled. The Jews were closing in, and now the Lord was talking about leaving them - alone. In times of uncertainty like that, when we feel anxious, it can sometimes be useful to ask ourselves "what is the worst that could happen?". If they had asked themselves that question, the answer would probably have been something along these lines: "The Lord will be captured, and the Jews will convince the Romans to execute Him. He will be killed but He is the Messiah and is destined to reign. It is all under the control of sovereign God."

And so the worst that could happen, if they really thought about it, was that Jesus would be killed, but would come back to life again so He could reign in glory. So the worst case scenario was actually the best case scenario. But they didn't think it through, and neither do we generally. Our instincts take over.

The Storm

A third example is how Jesus faced crises, of which His life was full. Yet He never got upset or uptight. He wasn't a worrier. He never had a panic attack, even though people were constantly out to defeat Him. When they were on thet storm on the Sea of Galilee (Matt.8:23-27), the disciples were petrified. They thought their lives were in jeopardy. Yet the Lord was sleeping in the boat. So they woke Him up and asked Him the same question that Martha had: "Don't you care?". As if He didn't care. And so He got up, calmed them down first and then calmed the storm. They must have asked one another "Where does He get His calmness from?"

On His last night, in the upper room, He gave them the answer. He said to them that He was going away and that He was going to give them the calmness that He had, because they'd need it. *"My peace I give to you; not as the world gives do I give to you"* (Jn.14:27). And so He gave them a source of peace quite different from how the world tries to relieve worry. It's peace of mind - as a gift of God. It's given to those who are already at peace 'with' God and it *"surpasses understanding"* (Phil.4:7). If you can explain where it came from, it's not the peace of God. God is the *"God of peace"* (Rom.15:33).

Peter, for one, must have understood. In Acts chapter 12 a few years later, he was in prison, chained to two guards, due to be executed the next day. How much sleep would we have had that night? But Peter was asleep; He had the peace of God. And It was Peter who told us how to obtain it: *"Casting all your care on Him, for He cares for you"* (1 Pet.5:7). "Lord, don't you care?" Oh yes, He cares. If it matters to us, it matters to Him. We need to give the burden to Him in prayer and then leave it there, trusting.

Is It That Important?

Isaiah 26:3 says, *"You will keep Him in perfect peace whose mind is stayed on you".* When we are feeling anxious about something, we need to step back and ask ourselves: "Why is it so important that it's making me feel this way?". Because what we think is important is a matter of our choice. If it's something legitimate, hasn't our heavenly Father promised to provide it, in His way and time? And so why am I trying to control it? And if it's not legitimate, why am I seeking it at all? It's making me ill - literally. If my mind was "stayed" on the Lord's things, I wouldn't be seeking these illegitimate things; they wouldn't be so important to me. And so I'm not helpless at all. I can choose what's important and truly believe God's promise to me that *"My God shall supply all your need according to His riches in glory by Christ Jesus"* (Phil.4:19). As I begin to truly believe that, my anxiety will dissipate. Faith has triumphed over feelings again.

The Formula

The Promise

When Paul was in prison, after a life full of trouble and perplexity, speaking from personal experience he said:

> *"Be anxious for nothing, but in everything by prayer and sup-plication, with thanksgiving, let your requests be made known to God; and the peace of God, which surpasses all understand-ing, will guard your hearts and minds through Christ Jesus"* (Phil.4:6,7).

Note that these verses don't promise to give us whatever it is we're anxious about. What it promises is the gift of the peace of God, which is actually what we need most. If someone is fatally ill, for example, heal-ing is not their greatest need; peace of mind is. And that is what we are being promised here. Many believers have testified to it. But this peace is elusive and doesn't last for ever. And so this is a promise that we must come back to time and time again, as new things occur to make us anxious.

Supplication

One of the necessary ingredients in this formula for peace of mind is "supplication". Consider for example if we were planning a big event (such as a wedding) and we were very stressed over all the things that had to be done before the big day. Suppose then that a trusted, capable friend came along, listened to all the details and then said, "Leave it all to me; I'll look after it". And you knew they would, and knew they'd do it at least as well as you would. How would you feel? What a sense of relief you would feel. You would have transferred your burden to them - cast your cares on them. That is what the Lord is offering whenever we're stressed.

And so when these verses refer to "supplication", it's not talking about a quick summary prayer, so that we can get back to our worrying. It's telling the Lord all the details. That's what supplication is. That's what Hannah did in 1 Samuel 1:10,11, in great distress over her childlessness: "*I have poured out my soul to the Lord*". She got it all out and gave it to Him, and then she felt a lot better.

Thankfulness

There is another vital ingredient in this formula that can easily be overlooked when we are seeking the peace of God. It's the two words "*with thanksgiving*". It's very important to God that people have an attitude of gratitude towards Him. 1 Thessalonians 5:18 says, "*In everything give thanks; for this is the will of God in Christ Jesus for you*". One of the things that makes God angry with people (according to Romans 1:21) is "*and were not thankful*". Thanksgiving should be characteristic of us; that's one way that God is praised. And so when we come to God in prayer and supplication at times when we're anxious, we should think of the many ways in which God has blessed us, how He has preserved us from things being a lot worse than they are. And we should thank Him for that. It will change our own attitude, and it will give us confidence in the God we're praying to.

Psychologists sometimes use the term "incompatible behaviour". To break a bad habit, they suggest devising a behaviour that is incompatible with it, so that we can't be doing both at the same time. Anxiety and thanksgiving are like that. We can't be worried and thankful at the same time. And so, when we get anxious, as we examine what it is that we have chosen to make so important that it has us stressed out, as we tell the Lord all about it and ask Him to take it all over, we begin to express thankfulness for all the things we do have, and for all the reminders of the bountiful goodness of God. We can then expect the peace of God to begin flowing, to calm us. Although we won't be able to explain it, the relief will be wonderful. Again, our faith in the promises of God will have triumphed over our negative feelings.

"God has not given us a spirit of fear" (2 Tim.1:7).

10. DEALING WITH LOW SELF-ESTEEM

"I can do all things through Christ who strengthens me" (Phil.4:13).

In 2 Samuel 9 we read the story of Mephibosheth, the son of Jonathan, David's great friend. David had made a covenant with Jonathan before he died, and now David wanted to fulfill it by showing kindness to his son. But Mephibosheth's response was *"What is your servant, that you should look upon such a dead dog as I am"*. That sounds like what we would call low self-esteem, a poor self-image. Maybe it because he was disabled, crippled in both feet. Or maybe it was because of how shabbily his grandfather Saul had treated David. But David received him whole-heartedly, gave him an estate and staff of his own, a permanent place at the king's table, and treated him as his own son. It was total acceptance. And when he was sitting at the king's table, no one could see his feet.

How do you feel about yourself? Do you like yourself as a person? Do you ever wish you were someone else? Many people suffer from low self-esteem, a poor self-image. They feel insecure, inadequate, inferior. They lack self-confidence.

The Effects of Low Self-esteem

One sign of low self-esteem is living constantly in fear - fear of the "real me" being found out, or fear of failure. This might be exhibited by frequent "I can't" language, or fear of being rejected ("I'm not good enough; I don't belong"). It can cause us to be timid and shy, withdrawn, and risk-averse.

Another sign can be frequently seeking other people's approval and recognition. An example is a wife (or husband) who keeps asking their spouse "do you love me?", rather than declaring to them "I love you".

73

They need that constant reassurance; it's called "deficit motivation" - being motivated to act out of a sense that's something's lacking in them. When two people plan to marry primarily based on a need to get love and acceptance and affirmation, based on feelings of inadequacy, rather than to give it, it's a danger sign. It can also be seen in reacting very negatively to any implied criticism, being hyper-sensitive and easily offended. Sometimes we would rather be ruined by praise than helped by constructive criticism.

A third sign of low self-esteem is over-compensating behaviour. Here the person becomes aggressive and assertive, as a cover-up for their feelings of inadequacy. They may try to manipulate others to make them act in a certain way or try to make them feel guilty. They may always have to appear to be right, to be the expert in the situation. They may belittle others or their achievements, rationalizing them away, in an attempt to build themselves up in their own mind. However it manifests itself, feeling inadequate can cripple our effectiveness. We were not meant to live that way.

What Causes Feelings of Inadequacy?

We were not born with feelings of inadequacy. No new-born infant in the crib suffers from a poor self-image. It's something we learn as we grow up. It's generally the result of two factors. One is frequent criticism, put-downs, being told we're not good enough and won't amount to anything, perhaps being bullied. After a while we begin to believe it ourselves ("They must know something I don't know. They must be right; I'm not very good.") And those painful early memories can be very hard to shake.

The other factor is our own tendency to compare ourselves with others. The apostle Paul spoke in 2 Corinthians 10:12 about people who "*measuring themselves by themselves, and comparing themselves among themselves, are not wise.*" We live in a competitive world. In sports there are winners and losers, and only one champion; everyone else "failed". In school we are graded on a relative scale; there are always people who get better grades than us. There are always people who are better at doing certain things. We often fail when we try something for the first time (because of the learning curve). This can undermine our confidence and cause us to be concerned about how others view us. Or perhaps we've lived under the shadow of an older brother or sister. Whatever the cause, we need to remember the saying "You wouldn't worry so much about what people think of you if you realized how seldom they do".

Because of our inner dialogue, which we discussed previously, we can tend to label ourselves by what we think we're good at and what we're not. And so a feeling of low self-esteem can become very ingrained and hard to overcome.

Performance and Reputation

One of Satan's deceptions is that our self-worth is the result of our performance and of other people's opinions of us. To the extent we fall for his ploy, it can lead to either compulsive or passive behaviour. Compulsive behaviour is the intense "I have to" mentality, where we're driven; we can't relax; we always have to prove ourselves. For example, we may convince ourselves "I have to work harder"; "I have to say just the right thing"; "I have to be in control"; It's all about performance and being "successful". These people can sometimes be perfectionists; anything less than perfection in what they do (which is an impossible standard to live up to) undermines their feeling of self-worth.

Passive behaviour, on the other hand, involves withdrawing, avoiding failure by avoiding risks, taking the safe path, staying within safe relationships, and avoiding having to be accountable. In extreme cases it can involve withdrawing into a fantasy world, where we can be successful in our own imaginations. An example is excessive use of video games, especially by boys and young men. One especially dangerous form is pornography, especially for males, where they look to this for gratification to avoid real relationships. Passive people with low self-esteem may appear easy-going, but they don't feel that way inside.

The reality is that our worth does not depend either on how well we perform or on what others think of us.

False Humility

Aren't Christians told to not think a lot of themselves? Isn't humility a Christian virtue, and pride a sin? Doesn't Romans 12:3 instruct us: *"not to think of himself more highly than he ought to think"*? Yes. But is it possible to think of yourself 'less' highly than you ought to think? That verse says we are to think "soberly" (with sound judgment) - that is, not over-estimating nor under-estimating ourselves.

In Matthew 22:39 the Lord said that we are to love our neighbour *"as our self"*. He takes it for granted that we love ourselves; that is proper; we are to love others just as much. Ephesians 5:29 says that no one ever hated his own flesh; it's a statement of fact. Even if you don't like the way you look, you care about how you look, which proves the point. Paul says that a good basis of a marriage is the husband loving his wife the way he does himself.

Humility does not consist in putting ourselves down; it's consists in not focusing on yourself. Christ was a meek and humble person, but He didn't go around talking about His own inadequacies, obviously. We don't have to dislike ourselves to be humble. In fact, constantly drawing attention to our weaknesses is a disguised form of pride. People with proper self-esteem can take the focus off themselves and put it on other people. If we don't accept ourselves, it will be hard to feel that others accept us, and that will make it hard for us to give of ourselves unconditionally.

The Example of Moses

Moses was a man who was described at the end of his life (in Num.12:3) as the meekest man on earth. But he wasn't always that way. Early on he was very aggressive; he committed murder and had to escape the country. Then he went to the other extreme and became a recluse in the wilderness of Sinai. When God came to call him to his life work, he was passive and reluctant. He was full of excuses. Five times he tried to get out of it on the basis that he wasn't good enough. Hadn't he tried once and failed miserably? He just wasn't up to God's plan.

But for each excuse God gave him an answer that He would personally make up the shortfall:

- Firstly: "Who am I that I should go?"; the answer: "I will be with you".
- Secondly: "Who are you?"; answer: "I am who I am ... the eternal God".
- Thirdly: "What if they won't believe me?"; the answer: "I will stretch out my hand and strike Egypt with all my wonders".
- Fourthly: "I'm not very articulate; I can't speak very well"; the answer: "Who made your mouth? I'll tell you what to say."
- Fifthly: "Use somebody else"; the answer: "Since if you insist; I'll use your brother instead."

What was the answer to him feeling inadequate? It was that God through Moses would be invincible.

What's the Remedy?

Eleanor Roosevelt once said that "Nobody can make you feel inferior without your consent." God does not intend us to live with low self-esteem and all its consequences. And He makes available to us, because we are "in Christ", all the means necessary to overcome it. He doesn't do it by changing our natural abilities and make us more adequate that way. He intends that our needs always be met in Him. That's why He made us with those needs - so that a proper relationship with Him would be the key to our lives.

Since low self-esteem is all in our minds, although very real, it's our thinking that has to change. We have to replace the false notions that we've learned growing up to the reality of God's Word. Again, it's faith over feelings.

Total Acceptance

Ephesians 1:6 says "*[by] His grace ... He has made us accepted in the Beloved*". This is what we are looking for - total acceptance; no fear of rejection. God has said unequivocally that, because we are "in Christ", we are completely accepted by Him, just as Mephibosheth was. He treats us as His own Son. He never sees us apart from Christ; He sees us as permanently "in Christ". And how does He think of Christ - with total approval, total acceptance, total love. And that's how He regards us now.

We each need to let that truth sink deep in. If other people see me differently, that's their problem. Who is right - God or them? This is the wonder of my justification - His righteousness becomes mine; His worth becomes mine. Is that real to us? God doesn't love us because we are good; we need His love in order to be good. Colossians 1:21,22 says that Christ will present us as "*beyond reproach in His sight*". This isn't a self-help program; this is present reality.

Total Adequacy

Colossians 2:10 says, "*In Him dwells all the fullness of the godhead bodily; and you are complete in Him*". When Moses was giving his excuses, when he felt he didn't measure up, he was assured that he wasn't by

Himself. With God he was invincible. In Colossians 2:10 we are being told we are now "complete in Him" - there is nothing lacking. Again it is a truism, not an aspiration.

Everything God intends us to accomplish in life, everything He saved us for, He has already equipped us for. 1 Peter 4:11 says, "*If anyone speaks, let him speak as the oracles of God. If anyone ministers, let him do it as with the ability which God supplies, that in all things God may be glorified through Jesus Christ*". When it's done with the ability God supplies, He gets the glory - which is the way it's meant to be. That's why God doesn't choose super-stars to do His work. Paul understood that. That's why he said in Philippians 4:13 that "*I can do all things through Christ who strengthens me.*" That's the way out of the "performance trap". If our view of ourselves is different from God's view of me, then it's our view that needs to change.

Total Significance

Ephesians 1:4 says: "*He chose us in Him before the foundation of this world*". How important are we to God? We are each just an integral part of His eternal purpose, that's all. He sent His Son to give up His life for us. He has made us His own son or daughter. He selected us to share Christ's glory - for ever. He wants us to be part of that select group of individuals who will be Christ's inheritance for all eternity - what God has given to Him. We are God's gift to His Son. How important is that? And yet we can be worried about my self-esteem? Paul said in 2 Corinthians 12:9,10: "*Most gladly I will rather boast in my infirmities, that the power of Christ may rest upon me. Therefore I take pleasure in infirmities, in reproaches, in needs, in persecutions, in distresses, for Christ's sake. For when I am weak, then I am strong.*" Paul had it right.

11. DEALING WITH DEPRESSION AND DISCOURAGEMENT

"Who can bear a broken spirit?" (Prov.18:14).

Depression is a sense of uncontrollable hopelessness. The intensity of the feeling can fluctuate from day to day or even hour by hour. It brings a sense of darkness, discouragement, doubt, despair and confusion. If we are depressed we feel unable to cope with even ordinary duties and tasks that we are well equipped to handle. We generally get little or no joy out of what we do.

What Causes Depression?

There are several potential causes of severe discouragement or depression, which can sometimes occur in combinations:

Inner Conflict

Depression can be the result of deep inner conflict, such as "cognitive dissonance" - which is a conflict between two incompatible life goals. It can also be the result of unresolved guilt. It can also be the result of being the victim of abusive behaviour in our youth. Severe childhood abuse (such as rape, incest, or pedophilia) can leave huge emotional scars, resulting in anger, depression (including severe mood swings), a sense of fear and vulnerability (resulting in extreme reactions to criticism), and a controlling personality (in an attempt to protect against additional hurt). These do not go away easily.

Inability to Control Circumstances

People with a controlling personality may be especially subject to depression when they are unable to control their circumstances. In Psalm 32:3-5 David said: *"When I kept silent, my bones grew old through my groaning all the day long. For day and night Your hand was heavy up-*

on me; my vitality was turned into the drought of summer. Selah. I ac-
knowledged my sin to You, and my iniquity I have not hidden." He was
depressed.

Physical causes

Depression is a feeling which can often be partly or largely attributable
to physical causes, such as hormone imbalance, neurological disorder,
lack of sleep, improper diet, drugs, glandular disorders, or blood chemical malfunctioning. Post-partum depression (a mother's depression after childbirth) is largely hormonal, and can be medicated to some extent, although it can last for many months and can be extremely serious. Research indicates that the hypothalamus part of the brain is often involved in depression. Some people may be genetically more prone
to depression, although depression itself is not inherited. Even where
the causes are physical, psychological factors may make it worse, or may
make the person more prone to it.

Past experiences

The feelings of inadequacy, hopelessness, unworthiness, self-pity and
self-blame that are associated with severe depression can be the result
of many experiences in our past. These can include:

(a) the futility of being unable to achieve a goal, no matter
how hard we try;

(b) grief at the loss of a loved one, since we cannot bring
them back;

(c) negative thinking - seeing life as just a series of burdens,
obstacles and defeats, with the future being even bleaker;

(d) a major loss - of a job, of health, of freedom, of valued possessions, of important people through divorce or separation; or

(e) an attitude of perfectionism, setting unrealistically high standards of performance for ourselves.

Feeling hurt

Suppressed anger can also lead to depression. It festers "under cover". When we are hurt, we can hide or replace the feelings of hurt with anger. We can then hide the anger by feeling a desire for revenge. This can lead to aggression, to physical symptoms or to depression. This can in turn involve feelings of guilt, and the depression then becomes a form of self-punishment.

The Effects of Depression

Like other problems, depression can occasionally have some short-term positive paybacks, such as time off work, excuse for avoiding responsibility, or sympathy from other; however, these tend eventually to back-fire. We come to hate what we are doing and thus hate ourselves, and so the depression deepens. Depression can lead to lack of enthusiasm, indecisiveness, lack of energy, putting on a veneer, and escapism. At the extreme, it can lead to suicidal attempts, which is the ultimate escape. Unsuccessful suicide attempts can also be a cry for help, an opportunity for revenge or an act of manipulation. They should always be taken seriously.

The Case of Elijah

An example of someone in the Bible who had depression is the prophet Elijah. He thought he was fighting the Lord's battle against the Baal-worshippers alone and was exasperated at the vacillation of God's people Israel. He had to run for his life, and he escaped into isolation in the wilderness and prayed that he might die. He felt he was a failure *("I am no better than my fathers"* - 1 Kin.19:4). God first addressed his physical needs. Through an angel He fed him (twice), caused him to get some sleep (twice), and then brought him away from his environment to Horeb. There God revealed Himself to Elijah, corrected his wrong thinking (*"I have reserved seven thousand in Israel, all whose knees have not bowed to Baal"* - 1 Kin.19:18), and commissioned him to take action to further continue His work. Elijah realized God hadn't forsaken him and had further plans for him. He got him "off the sidelines and back in the game".

Dealing with Depression

Diagnosis of depression involves identifying the underlying causes, which often requires tracing it to its early occurrences. Where there is an underlying medical condition, a medical doctor should be consulted. People do not just "snap out of it". The recovery process is usually long and irregular. If a counselor is involved, they may need to protect the person from harming themselves in the meantime.

12. AN INTRODUCTION TO PART TWO

This section of the book is not about psychological therapy. Nor is it an in-depth prescription for dealing with particular or advanced cases of personal difficulty. It is intended to be a helpful guide for mature Christians who have a sincere desire to help other believers resolve issues and difficulties in their lives according to the Word of God. Providing such assistance is not just the domain of highly-trained experts. God has ordained that disciples of the Lord Jesus should not live in isolation from each other, but should be a source of strength and encouragement to each other. God often uses His people to be means whereby the resources which are available in Christ can flow to each other. That is how the Body of Christ functions.

When we first attempt to become involved in trying to assist others in this way, we can easily feel quite helpless. We can become very aware that the difficulties are serious, and perhaps well beyond our knowledge and experience to address. We may have a real concern that we may inadvertently say the wrong thing or give bad advice, and so make matters worse. We might find ourselves at stages in the conversation not knowing what to say next. This uncomfortable experience can actually spur us on develop a greater understanding of how to be a biblical counselor in a wide variety of situations where we are called on or have opportunity to help. It is for people such as this that this booklet is intended.

We might assume that Biblical counseling only applies to the so-called "spiritual" areas of our lives - our service for God. We may think that that the difficulties we face in other areas, such as marriage, other interpersonal relationships, illness, addiction, job and financial stress, and grief lie outside the scope of such help. But the life that we have been called to and equipped to live for the Lord is all-encompassing. The scriptures are relevant and sufficient in giving us the principles we need in order to deal with problems in all area of our lives. Compartmentalizing our lives, and only looking to the Word of God for solutions in some areas, will severely inhibit the work of God in bringing in the fullness of the life He has given us. Spiritual maturity involves acquiring the wisdom from the Word of God to apply to each situation in life. As we do that in faith, our conviction about its truth and applicability increases.

"His divine power has given to us all things that pertain to life and godliness" (2 Peter 1:3).

13. QUESTIONS ABOUT COUNSELING

"If you abide in My word, you are My disciples indeed. And you shall know the truth, and the truth shall make you free" (Jn.8:31,32).

What is Counseling?

Counseling is having one or more conversations with someone in an attempt to help them deal with a difficult problem or make a difficult decision; in terms, it is a way to help each other's on-going sanctification. It is a process, not an event. The skills are applicable to a variety of situations. Another person can often help us see ourselves and our circumstances more objectively. We can learn a lot about ourselves by disclosing ourselves to another person.

There are many types of counselors in the world these days - psychologists, social workers, therapists, etc. Even Christian counselors do not all use biblical counseling - counseling based firmly on the Word of God. Great care should therefore be used in using or referring someone to a counselor who is not using a Bible-based approach.

What is 'Christian' Counseling?

Christian counseling is simply counseling based of the Word of God, on the grounds that it is relevant and sufficient for all personal problems, not just so-called "spiritual" ones. There are several underlying premises of Christian counseling, that are very different from secular counseling – for example:

(a) we are morally accountable to the true God (vs. God is an impersonal force);

(b) we are sinful creatures, which alienates us from God (vs. man is basically good);

(c) the necessary and only remedy for all sin is the sacrifice of Christ, which is made available to us freely through our faith (vs. there is no such thing as objective sin or moral guilt);

(d) by participating in the benefits of the work of Christ through faith we receive the Holy Spirit, who gives us the power we need to deal with all our personal circumstances (vs. redemption is the realization that my negative self-assessment is not true);

(e) the truth from God is found in the Word of God, which is applicable and sufficient for all our personal needs (vs. the answer to our problems is realizing our own subjective reality); and

(f) the goal of counseling is holiness, our relationship to the Lord and our usefulness to Him (vs. the goal is personal feelings of happiness on any basis).

"All Scripture is given by inspiration of God, and is profitable for doctrine, for reproof, for correction, for instruction in righteousness, that the man of God may be complete, thoroughly equipped for every good work" (2 Tim.3:16).

Christian counseling is concerned with whether or not we are responding obediently to whatever situation is being experienced. As counselors we are just instruments in the hand of God who wants to change people's lives (it's part of their on-going sanctification).

The goals of Christian counseling are to help people:

(a) function more effectively in their daily lives,

(b) find freedom from spiritual, psychological and interpersonal conflicts,

(c) be at peace with themselves,

(d) enjoy a growing communion with God,

(e) develop and maintain smooth interpersonal relationships with others,

(f) realize their fullest potential in Christ, and

(g) be actively involved in becoming disciples, and disciplers, of Jesus Christ

What is Secular or Non-Biblical Counseling?

Bible-based counseling and secular counseling are fundamentally different, although some of the skills applied are similar. Christian counseling recognizes the spiritual dimension of people. However not all Christian counselors use the Bible as the foundation of their counseling, either because of their secular training or because they may relegate the Bible to "spiritual" principles outside the realm of real-life personal problems. Great care must therefore be taken in the choice of the counselor being used, and in the approach they take. For example, sometimes the counselor (even a "Christian" one) may regard the person's problem to be partly attributable to their Christianity or to their church affiliation, and advise them to leave it. This is clearly not a solution for a disciple in a church of God.

Here are some of the differences:

- Secular counseling generally has as its goal the person's

happiness, on whatever basis that can be achieved. Whatever helps to overcome feelings of unhappiness is regarded as positive. Biblical counseling, on the other hand, has the goal of personal holiness, involving obedience to the will of God, a closer relationship with the Lord Jesus and living in the power of the Holy Spirit, of which true happiness is a real by-product.

- Secular counseling does not generally regard human beliefs and behaviour as moral issues relative to a God to whom we are accountable. It does not consider the factor of sin or that some behaviour is sinful, and the need for confession and repentance in a person's life as a remedy for sinful behaviour – a process which the biblical counselor knows cannot be by-passed, or else it will have repercussions later.

- Secular counseling does not base hope for change and a better future on the promises of God, based on the sacrifice of Christ and our relationship as being "in" Him. It does not acknowledge the Holy Spirit as being the source of the power to transform thinking and behaviour, and to produce positive feelings as His "fruit" in peoples' lives. The biblical counselor recognizes that only the Holy Spirit in the believer can bring about real change in their life. The biblical counselor will not only counsel and encourage the person but will pray for (and perhaps with) them also, in recognition of these dependencies.

- Secular counseling relies on conventional worldly wisdom and does not acknowledge the Bible as being the source of "truth" which is absolute and relevant to all problems people face. The biblical counselor recognizes that only the Word of God presents absolute truth, and therefore tests everything against scripture, wisely applying scriptural principles to the particular situation.

Some humanistic therapeutic approaches can be summarized as follows, based on which part of the person they focus on:

(a) The body – all problems are due to malfunctions of the body. Many psychiatrists, for example, rely largely on medication.

(b) The emotions – they help people to "get in touch with their true feelings, and "find the inner resources" to feel good about themselves.

(c) The will – they help feel to face their responsibility and consequences of their actions (which is appropriate), but they regard "sin" as just an offense against others' and their own values.

(d) Patterns of relating (e.g. "transactional analysis") – people learn "life scripts" as children which they act out in adult life. Awareness of their "ego state" as "child" (uninhibited or fearfully conforming), "adult" (analytical and unemotional) or "parent" (nurturing or controlling/disciplining) is believed to allow positive changes to occur.

(e) The mind – an inner conviction of self-worth leads to positive thinking; negative self-image leads to attempts to master their personal environment, often by destructive behaviour.

See Appendix 1 for a brief history of psychology.

"... there is no wisdom or understanding or counsel against the LORD" (Prov.21:30).

Who is Able to Counsel Biblically?

It is a realistic aspiration for every reasonably spiritually mature Christian to develop a certain level of competence in this area, as we saw from Romans 15:14. For example, Galatians 6:1,2 states: *"If a man is overtaken in any trespass, you who are spiritual restore such a one in a spirit of gentleness".* Restoring a disciple who has encountered some difficulties requires a care and a degree of competence. But it does not necessarily require professional training. Some Christians are specially gifted in this area, and included among the spiritual gifts which the Holy Spirit provides to believers is the one referred to as helps: *"God has appointed these in the church ... helps ..."* (1 Cor.12:28). It would appear therefore that God has specially gifted some brethren and sisters in churches of God to be particularly capable in the area of people-helping, if they develop their gift. As with other spiritual gifts, it can be discerned over time through sensing the Lord placing a burden on their heart to help their brothers and sisters who are in present difficulty, and by seeing evidence of the Lord working through them to their blessing when they do engage in it.

Because of the on-going need for such assistance, brothers and sisters who sense that they may have been gifted for a ministry to others in the assemblies are urged to develop that capability through use and study. This may involve more than just the general principles and skills of counseling, but also the particulars of specific types of problems that they may encounter.

The following verses include the word "admonish", which can be a component of biblical counseling:

> *"Let the word of Christ dwell in you richly in all wisdom, teaching and admonishing one another in psalms and hymns and spiritual songs, singing with grace in your hearts to the Lord"* (Col.3:16).

"I myself am confident concerning you, my brethren, that you also are full of goodness, filled with all knowledge, able also to admonish one another" (Rom.15:14).

The word 'admonish' (Greek: 'noutheto') is a word meaning both instructing and warning. Paul expressed confidence that those saints in the church in Rome were both sufficiently knowledgeable and properly motivated to do that for each other. It was not that one class of saints were always the counselors and the rest always needed the help; any one of them could be on either side of that process from time to time. Paul described a woman named Phoebe in that assembly as a people-helper in this way - "she has been a helper of many and of myself also" (Rom.16:2). While we don't know the details of the help she gave, it is notable that she was even a helper to the apostle.

However, where there may be physical or organic causes or effects of the problem, referral should be made to a medical doctor (scripture supports the use of medical doctors). In very difficult cases of mental malfunction, the person may be referred to an experienced or professional counselor, but with great care.

"Therefore comfort each other and edify one another, just as you also are doing" (1 Thess.5:11).

"There is no wisdom or understanding or counsel against the LORD" (Prov.21:30).

When Should I Decline to Counsel and/or Make a Referral?

Sometimes it will be appropriate to suggest to the person that they receive assistance from someone else - either a professional counselor or another mature Christian. This may be done at the outset, or it may be done after working with them for some time. Referral to another counselor is not a cure for the person's lack of co-operation, but it can be a cure for lack of success. Nor is it just a way to avoid having to become involved yourself.

Any true disciple of Christ who is willing to be helped from the scriptures, and who is willing to co-operate and attempt the required changes, can be counseled. Normally however, family members should not be counseled in this way (other than parents exercizing their parental responsibility to their children), because of their lack of objectivity and the inherent conflict of interest due to the family relationship which can interfere with the process. It will often be preferable to recommend that someone else provide the counseling. Also, no one who is part of the problem, or who has a similar unresolved problem of their own, should attempt to provide counseling.

There are dangers in attempting to counsel non-believers in Christ to live biblically, since they do not accept the fundamental basis on which Christian counseling is carried out. They first need to be brought to a relationship of acknowledging Christ as their Saviour and Lord, since this is a pre-requisite for the biblical counseling process. It can be dangerous to counsel them before they are saved because they may try to substitute human reformation for spiritual transformation, or have false assurance about their spiritual condition, and be set up for failure.

If the problem is beyond your capabilities or experience, refer the person to a specialist or someone more experienced, if possible. This includes cases of severe relationship, mental or emotional problems. Also, where any physical causes or symptoms, including stress, become apparent, the person should be advised to consult a medical doctor for these aspects. Counseling for other aspects can continue.

Be very careful before referring a believer to a secular counselor, or even to a Christian counselor who does not use a biblically-sound approach (see below). Once a professional counselor has accepted the person as a client, you need the person's permission to give any details to that counselor, to protect their privacy.

What are the Ingredients for Successful Counseling?

In 1 Thessalonians 5:14, Paul said to the church: "we exhort you, brethren, warn those who are unruly, comfort the fainthearted, uphold the weak, be patient with all". He was indicating to them that not all situations call for the same approach, that there is a diversity in what the need is, how the counseling is to be provided, and that the counselor needs to be sensitive to each individual case. This isn't "one size fits all".

Having said that, counseling is not just telling people what to do or giving them advice. Research indicates that imposing authority or just using human logic has a low frequency of lasting success. It increases people's resistance. If it works at all, it tends to just result in routine compliance and not heartfelt lasting change. The style that has been shown to be by far the most effective is collaboration, where the person and the counselor work together to discover the underlying problem and the proper remedy. Collaboration generally takes longer than other methods, but it is far more effective.

This approach requires that the counselor provide a high level of support throughout the entire process. Without that, the person will be unlikely to open up and express themselves or respond to guidance. They will be far less likely to be willing to take the risks inherent in attempting changes in behaviour. However, being collaborative is not the same as being passive. At some point in the process the counselor needs to gently but firmly challenge the person's thinking. This is actually the point at which the real counseling itself begins. People generally appreciate honest confrontation as long as they don't feel punished or threatened by it.

Two major elements that will affect a person's willingness to be helped are rapport with the counselor and confidentiality. Rapport involves being approachable and empathetic. Confidentiality and trust are vital, or else people will not open up and disclose how they really feel. For this reason, some people will not accept help from someone with whom they have another on-going relationship. They feel it would be too difficult to reveal inner problems and behaviour and then continue to have regular contact with them.

Also, for a counseling intervention to be successful, the person seeking help must be prepared to:

(a) be honest with themselves and the counselor;

(b) acknowledge that they have a problem that needs to be resolved, even if the situation isn't fair or of their making;

(c) co-operate with the counselor and want to change;

(d) take responsibility for themselves and not blame other people or things for their problem;

(e) be guided by the Word of God, even where it conflicts with their present attitudes or actions; and

(f) put in the effort and time, including work between counseling sessions.

14. THE PROCESS OF COUNSELING - INTRODUCTION

"You will guide me with Your counsel" (Ps.73:24).

Counseling is more than just trying to comfort someone, to make them feel better, or even exhorting them to change their behaviour. The objective of any Biblical counseling intervention is to bring about change towards more godly living. In most cases it takes much more than merely pointing out the error of their ways and showing them the scriptures which describe how they ought to be living. It involves helping the person, largely through conversation, to understand the wrong thinking and beliefs that are leading to their difficulty, and then attempting them to move over to appropriate biblical thinking and actions. This is often a very difficult process, because people do not generally change ingrained beliefs easily.

Even committed Christians, when confronted with the clear word of scripture, may mentally agree with it but not necessarily internalize it sufficiently; or they may convince themselves they are acting according to what it says, when really they're not. Change is difficult, especially when someone else is expecting us to do the changing. Usually there is no short-cut to the process, and the counselor must be prepared to patiently invest the time required. It also requires both a working knowledge of scripture, and wise application of it in particular circumstances. Knowledge and wisdom are both involved, and they are often linked with each other in scripture.

How to Begin

Counseling may be initiated at the invitation of the person wishing help, by an offer by the potential counselor, or at the instigation of an interested third party. People who ask for counseling usually do so because of problem feelings – they feel unhappy. Their unhappiness moti-vates them to want things to be different, but they may not know how to change, or else think they lack the strength. Whether or not they do ask for help depends on several factors, such as: their perception of the seriousness of the problem, whether they know of a counselor who can help them and with whom they will feel comfortable, whether they feel they can be helped, the cost, and whether they are prepared to invest the necessary time and emotional energy.

However it may occur, counseling can only proceed with the person's consent. The initial approach must be very sensitive and positive, ex-pressing genuine love for them and concern for their well-being. If they sense an ulterior motive, they are unlikely to be willing to participate. Even where the problem is severe, the emotional energy required to confront it can be daunting, and some people prefer to stay in an un-happy "comfort zone" rather than venture out into the unknown.

Counseling Phases

It can be useful for the counselor to think of the total process as con-sisting of two main phases (diagnostic and change), although these will seldom be pursued systematically from start to end. Nor is this some-thing that necessarily needs to be advised to the person being helped.

A Counseling Model

The "OVER" Model

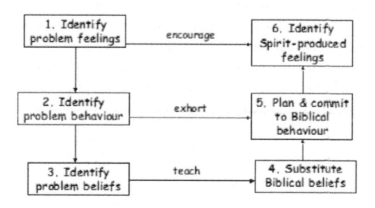

A model serves as a road-map for a counselor. This one is called the "OVER" model because it seeks to move the person's beliefs over to God's truth. The left side (steps 1 to 3) is the diagnostic phase, and the right side (steps 4 to 6) is the change phase. It is necessary to complete the left side before attempting the right side – on the principle: "Seek first to understand before trying to be understood". Not only does this give us a fuller understanding before we try to advise; it also tends to make the other person more willing to listen to us.

The three essential levels of this model are: (a) feelings (emotions); (b) behaviour (actions); and (c) beliefs (assumptions, thinking, attitudes, values). The sequence is important. Feelings should normally be addressed first, as unexpressed emotion can block the ability to engage in rational problem-solving. Also, expressing the feelings can reveal a lot about the underlying beliefs and wrong thinking. They are often the first to emerge in a conversation. People tend to talk readily about negative feelings; it shows how strongly they feel about the problem. A biblical example of this is at the death of Lazarus in John 11. The Lord let Martha, then Mary, express their grief and their confusion. He observed the grief of their friends, and wept with them, before acting.

Three Levels of Helping People

The model shows three levels of helping:

a. Encouraging

If we simply try to make someone feel better, but don't address wrong actions or assumptions, we are simply trying to encourage them. One way to do this is to broaden their perspective on their situation. Examples of this are comforting a sick person, and cheering up a disappointed person. Most people experiencing personal anguish can be greatly helped by the warm, genuine interest of people who care. We should avoid "pat" answers and instant solutions. Rather, we should stay a while, ask genuine questions and listen.

Encouragement only attempts to address the person's negative feelings. Anyone who cares enough can attempt to encourage someone else although their success will depend largely on the other person's willingness to be encouraged or comforted.

"... the God of all comfort, who comforts us in all our tribulation, that we may be able to comfort those who are in any trouble, with the comfort with which we ourselves are comforted by God" (2 Cor.1:3-4).

b. Exhorting

Exhortation in scripture usually has action in mind. It involves suggesting strongly to the person that they do something in particular. If their present choice of actions is based on wrong beliefs or assumptions, the exhortation to change is unlikely to be successful. If their present behaviour is sinful, we should not exhort them to new behaviour until they have first acknowledged and confessed their sin. Being able to exhort someone to behave in a godly way requires a working knowledge of scripture and its application to various situations.

> *"... we exhort you, brethren, warn those who are unruly, comfort the fainthearted, uphold the weak, be patient with all"* (1 Thess.5:14-15).

> *"... exhort one another daily ..."* (Heb.3:13).

c. Teaching

This is the deepest of the three levels and addresses not only feelings and behaviour, but probes into the person's underlying beliefs and thinking. Having identified erroneous beliefs, it then attempts to enlighten the person regarding the truth (of God from scripture), so as to replace the wrong beliefs. Having embraced the truth, they can then be guided how to replace wrong behaviour with behaviour which is incompatible with it.

> *"... the eyes of your understanding being enlightened; that you may know ..."* (Eph.1:18).

> *"A servant of the Lord must not quarrel but be gentle to all, able to teach, patient, in humility correcting those who are in opposition, if God perhaps will grant them repentance, so that they may know the truth, and that they may come to their senses and escape the snare of the devil, having been taken captive by him to do his will"* (2 Tim.2:24-26).

Teaching is instructing a person in the truth of God from scripture. It has as its aim that the Holy Spirit will enlighten the person and reveal to them and convict them of the truth and applicability of scripture to their situation. It often involves confronting wrong beliefs, assumptions and attitudes. For lasting change, most counseling needs to go to this depth.

15. THE PROCESS OF COUNSELING – THE DIAGNOSTIC PHASE

Key principle: "Seek first to understand before seeking to be understood"

"The heart of the prudent acquires knowledge; and the ear of the wise seeks knowledge" (Prov.18:15).

The purpose of the first phase is diagnosis. By means of questions and answers the counselor seeks to draw the person out and have them describe how they are feeling and the thinking that gave rise to it. This may take some time and may not be completed in a single session. It is often painful for people to probe into the issues that are affecting their lives. The counselor must be very supportive and positive throughout this process and must give cause for hope, so that the person does not become discouraged and want to give up. We should do more listening than talking in this phase. We do not need to express agreement or disagreement with what is being said but may ask questions for clarification.

Depending on the situation, we may begin with asking either about the person's feelings or behaviour, but we should encourage them to express their feelings – to remove emotional barriers to problem-solving, and to obtain clues as to their underlying thinking. In data gathering, we shouldn't settle for generalizations; we should ask for particulars and, if necessary, for several examples. We need to gather enough information to truly understand the problem, or else there won't be a convergence between the person and us in the process.

We should attempt to understand it both from the person's viewpoint, and from God's (scripturally). We should deal with both relationships and issues; usually relationships have to be healed before the issues can be dealt with. We should establish explicitly the impact of the behaviour, and not consider it self-evident. Establishing the impact is necessary to get a commitment later; when it occurs, it is a "teachable moment".

In order to be in a position to influence the person to change, we may need to learn:

(a) what they value the most;

(b) their expectancies and beliefs;

(c) their fears, biases and prejudices;

(d) what positions they are most likely to accept or reject;

(e) if a strained relationship is involved, what they need to hear from the other person to conclude that the person can be trusted;

(f) what they consider relevant;

(g) how they feel about themselves; and

(h) what they want most in their lives.

If at any point we detect a lack of hope in the person, we must postpone what we are doing to work on generating hope. We can point to the certain promises of scripture. If at any time the person feels the situation is hopeless, they will stop participating in a meaningful way.

> "May the God of hope fill you with all joy and peace in believing, that you may abound in hope by the power of the Holy Spirit" (Rom.15:13).

We need to be assured early on that the person's goals and ours are both biblical – i.e. to do whatever God wants them to do about the problem. Ask them why they want to fix the problem. Repentance can't be a gimmick to get what they want. Many people talk as though their problems have no connection to Christ, and that God's job is just to get them out of the mess. However, Christ is not only in the solution, but in the problem itself. He wants to accomplish something good out of it (Rom.8:28) ("God is up to something good here; I wonder what it is?"). Ask how the problem has diminished their usefulness to God. Don't minimize the problem, or the person's negative self-evaluation; rather maximize the Saviour and what He can do.

We should be on the lookout for any indications that the person's problem has physical/organic causes, or that they need medical attention. We should recommend a medical checkup if necessary. Stress caused by the problem can also result in health problems and may require medical attention.

Inhibitors to Change

During this phase, it is important to uncover what patterns may be inhibiting the person from making the changes in their life that they need to. Some examples include:

a. Denial of the situation, rather than facing the reality of it, perhaps because it "isn't fair", or "this shouldn't be happening to me", or embarrassment.

b. Making assumptions, without testing them, because they want them to be true, and so misinterpreting the situation.

c. 'Perceptual defense', 'blind spots' – unconsciously blocking things out that would upset them.

d. Paralysis caused by fear.

e. "Deceptive masking" to make things appear other than they are (e.g. "toughing it out").

f. The pain of dealing with the problems; it "seems easier" not to.

g. Being prepared to compromise and settle for less ("it's not too bad"; "I can live with it").

h. Being more concerned about proving they're 'right' than solving the problem.

i. Arguing their limitations, to convince themselves they can't solve it.

j. Justifying themselves rather than seeking a solution.

k. Not being honest with themselves or with God.

They need to be shown that these strategies are not working. They need to be shown that excuses don't help. Problems don't get better with time. What they do not acknowledge will get worse until they do. Alcoholism is an example – if they don't face it, they won't replace it. They need to acknowledge what is not working in their life. "If they continue to do what they've always done, they will continue to have what they've always had." If they 'do' different, they will 'have' different. Most people do not want truth, they want validation – reinforcement for their present thinking, things that make them feel good. We treasure being right, and we spend a lot of time trying to convince others of that. Self-honesty means acknowledging the truth, the whole truth, even if it's ugly. It takes courage and commitment. Ignoring the truth won't change it. As a counselor we can ask "Can you handle the truth?".

The Importance of Personal History

A person's individual history can have a large bearing on their beliefs and attitudes, and thus on their behaviour. Many attitudes are deep-rooted from childhood, and are ingrained from their upbringing, their schooling, and interactions with peers. Criticism, bullying and abuse, for example, can have long-lasting effects. Victims of abuse, for example, can have great difficulty reconciling what happened with the goodness of God. It often helps to inquire into an early occasion when the person remembers feeling or doing something in particular. Quite often it may uncover "defining moments" in their upbringing which altered their beliefs and attitudes. Inquiring into what parents and grandparents did can yield clues.

It can be very tempting to try to speed up this process and jump to conclusions and quick remedies. But the experienced counselor will know that this phase has only been completed when both they and the individual fully understand the beliefs, the thinking and the assumptions that have led to their past behavior and to the feelings they are now experiencing. Also by this stage the person should hopefully be experiencing a certain amount of desire for change because they appreciate that the path they have been on is not a positive one. This discontent with the way things are is an important catalyst to moving them to the next phase. Someone has said: "When the pain of staying the same becomes greater than the pain of changing, we will change."

16. THE PROCESS OF COUNSELING - THE CHANGE PHASE

"... the truth shall set you free" (Jn.8:32).

The purpose of the second phase is to help the person to change their thinking to accord with the Word of God, and to make a commitment to specific actions that will put it into practice. This is a very difficult process because people do not easily change behaviour patterns and the way they react to circumstances. Even with the best of intentions it is very difficult for a mature person to change their fundamental beliefs, even where they can see that they are totally in accord with scripture, which they regard to be the authoritative Word of God. Mental acceptance is not enough, but it is an important first step.

Changing Beliefs

Once we as a counselor have learned everything we need to know about the problem we are ready to move the person 'over' to biblical thinking and action (step 4). This often involves changing the tone of the conversation, with us as counselor becoming more confrontational and more directive. Unless this point is reached at some stage in the process at which we disagree with the person, usually with respect to their thinking, we have no counsel to offer them; the point of disagreement is the point of hope at which counseling can begin (the bottom of the 'U' in the 'over' model). Scripture must be used directly here. This is where the teaching begins.

The ability to change beliefs according to the Word of God is given by the Holy Spirit. It is also the Spirit who convicts of sin. We should not progress to the next step until there is evidence that this divine work is taking place in the person. The counselor should seek assurance from the person that they do in fact see the truth of scripture as it applies to their situation.

Changing a deeply held belief is an act of faith, which activates the power of God within us. It is this exercize of faith that gives us the power to overcome the negative things in our life. The apostle John reported (in Jn.16:33) that the Lord Jesus said, *"In the world you will have tribulation; but be of good cheer, I have overcome the world."* John himself said in his first epistle (5:4): *"this is the victory that has overcome the world - our faith"*. He also tells us the two requirements for that to work:

(a) being born again, and thus having the Holy Spirit within us *"whatever is born of God overcomes the world"* - 1 Jn.5:4); and

(b) having scripture within us (*"the word of God abides in you and you have overcome the wicked one"* – 1 Jn.2:14).

"the word which they heard did not profit them, not being mixed with faith in those who heard it" (Heb.4:2-3).

Sometimes people feel trapped by past life experiences that were extremely damaging. They may be mistakes they made, for which they are still feeling guilt. Or they may have been victimized, such as by rape or abuse. The hurt from these experiences is very deep. But they need to realize that they are now responsible to deal with the present, to relinquish the control that the perpetrator or event still has over their life and choose to take that control back.

"... by whom a person is overcome, by him also he is brought into bondage" (2 Pet.2:19).

Sin and Repentance

This is the stage at which the person should discover the error of their thinking and behaviour. They need to recognize it as "sin", and that the only and proper remedy for sin is repentance and confession, relying on the sure promise of 1 John 1:9 for forgiveness and cleansing. Confession essentially means agreement; it should be accompanied by forsaking the sin. Always call sin "sin", rather than downplaying it. Names are important; they can point to solutions. It is doing no favour to a person to disguise sin as a sickness or genetic problem. Repentance (a change of mind and attitude to the behaviour) is something God gives (2 Tim.2:25).

"He who covers his sins will not prosper, but whoever confesses and forsakes them will have mercy" (Prov.28:13).

We need to realize that we are never going to be without problems and challenges in this life, and we are never going to become sinless *("If we say that we have no sin, we deceive ourselves, and the truth is not in us"* - 1 Jn.1:8). ("It's not whether you get knocked down; it's whether you get up" - Vince Lombardi.) If we realize this, we are less likely to react to every problem as a crisis.

Changing the Behaviour

Once the applicable truth of scripture has been truly assimilated, it is necessary to show the person how to put it into concrete action (step 5). This usually involves exchanging old habits for new ones. This takes time and repetition. It must be a conscious and deliberate choice, and it takes commitment, with accountability (e.g. "are you willing to do some things to change this?"). A counselor can help by (a) showing them not only what to do, but also how to do it; and (b) holding them accountable until the new behaviour becomes ingrained. Emphasize the person's obligation to fulfil God's commandments whether they feel like it or not. A lack of commitment may reveal that step (4) has not actually been fully completed, or that repentance has not really taken place. (Repentance is not just the desire to have the consequences altered.) Don't encourage unrepentant persons to attempt new behaviour.

Tell them not to wait until they feel like it; the blessing comes in doing (Jas.1:25). The feelings come after we do it (similar to engaging in a physical exercize workout). It is when the person doesn't feel like it that they especially need to commit to doing it. We need to help them to change their perspective (e.g. redefine success). Usually the motivation to change comes when the person is so "sick to death" of the problem that they reach the point of saying that they won't stand for it any longer, and they take charge of the need to solve it. We can help them to realize they have reached that point.

Changing their mind and conduct is a difficult thing. When it is us who are proposing the change, we tend to emphasize the benefits; when we are being asked to change, we tend to focus on the threats. They aren't going to like it at first (just as with physical training). It takes conscious resolve. It has to be done a step at a time. Some people are so embedded in a losing lifestyle that they have a comfort zone around it. To move out of that zone, even though it would overcome a long-standing problem may be too threatening for them. If this is the case, we need to increase our support for them taking that risk. People go through phases when asked to change:

(a) from contentment to denial,

(b) to confusion,

(c) to renewal, and

(d) to contentment again.

Undertaking step 5 (changing behaviour) reinforces three other steps in the process:

(a) It replaces the old behaviour (step 2) with incompatible behaviour;

(b) it deepens the conviction of the new beliefs (Jn.7:17); and

(c) it begins to produce the positive feelings (step 6), such as "love, joy and peace" (Gal.5:22).

That is why scripture places such emphasis on acting on our faith obediently. For example, we are told, on the basis of faith in God's word and not our feelings, to:

(a) *"love one another"* (Jn.13:34);

(b) *"forgive one another"* (Col.3:13); and

(c) *"be filled with the Spirit"* (Eph.5:18).

We are not told to pray for these things; we are told to do them – they are our responsibility. We are to "behave our way to success".

Intentions do no good, if not translated into action. Winners do things that losers don't want to do; therein lies the difference. It doesn't happen by accident. If they are vague about their intentions, we can ask them to put a verb in their sentence to make it action-oriented. Excuses and procrastination result in defeat. People at the end of their life frequently regret things they didn't do when they had the opportunity. Seizing the moment is important.

> *"A man had two sons, and he came to the first and said, 'Son, go, work today in my vineyard.' He answered and said, 'I will*

not,' but afterward he regretted it and went. Then he came to the second and said likewise. And he answered and said, 'I go, sir,' but he did not go. Which of the two did the will of his father?" They said to Him, "The first." (Matt.21:28-31).

To change from inaction to action requires them to have a conversation with themselves. Ask them to pose the questions and fears and get concrete answers back. "If you feel empty, give; it will fill you up." "If you need love from someone, then love someone."

Developing a Plan

Helping people to change their behaviour based on new beliefs involves helping them to develop a plan or strategy that they can follow. It's not enough just to tell them what to do; they must be shown how to do it. Don't create unrealistic expectations, but do ensure the action plan is specific, with accountabilities. Avoid lapsing into telling or persuading them. It must be their choice; they are responsible for their behaviour. Don't substitute your judgment for theirs. Do not accept the person's responsibilities for them. Don't make choices for them but confront them to make choices.

Getting a Commitment

The commitment should not be just compliance (going along with it) but real dedication to the plan of action. If getting this is a problem, reassess the first 4 steps, to see if any need to be repeated. Low commitment is often due to lack of belief in the problem definition, its impact and/or its likely success. Watch their body language. Be persistent (e.g. "I need to know where you are on this"). Clarify outcomes and consequences of the commitment.

Excuses and resistance need to be confronted. These are normal with change and can occur at any time in the process. Focus on what can be controlled (excuses vs. legitimate reasons). Make the resistance itself the topic of the conversation. Don't argue or debate with them. Ensure that your confronting their excuses is not interpreted as being non-supportive. Concentrate on future behaviour, not the past. Avoid a response of "I'll try"; it sets up an excuse for quitting; ask for a commitment to 'do it' for, say, 30 days. Don't accept excuses for not showing up at counseling sessions; when they feel least like it is when they need it the most.

At the End of Each Session

Homework assignments are useful at the end of each session for reinforcement; they must be concrete, not vague. Get a commitment to do them, and take them up carefully next time. Also, at the end of each session give the person some confidence and hope. The period between counseling sessions is important – for living up to commitments; looking for progress; and for not becoming dependent on you as the counselor. The person should be encouraged not to view the counseling sessions as the only times when change should occur.

Reinforcement

One of the biggest inhibitors to change can be the fear of failure, perhaps as a result of previous unsuccessful attempts. They may feel unable to maintain the discipline required to establish new habits and apply the change in thinking that they accept mentally. This is where the counselor may have a role to play in providing ongoing reinforcement. They may be able to recommend a suitable accountability partner for this purpose. This can be especially important where the change in behavior involves stopping some destructive behavior such as an addiction. It may require several periodic reviews to help the person stay on track. Bad habits die hard and new habits require repeated reinforcement to be established.

In his epistle James talks about the connection between faith and it works. 'Faith' is believing something deeply in our heart; it is something that we are convinced about. "Works' is the resulting behaviour that give evidence of the faith. Where the behavior or actions are inconsistent with scripture, the faith in the scripture is weak and needs to be strengthened. The counselor can propose small actions at first to reinforce the small amount of faith that is already there. As these are completed successfully they will reinforce the faith and more ambitious actions can be proposed. This cycle of reinforcement is often necessary in order to move someone over to a change in lifestyle which is based on a genuine application of the Word of God in their lives.

"I acknowledged my sin to You ... Blessed is he whose transgression is forgiven" (Ps. 32:5,1).

One of the differences between biblical and secular counseling is the recognition of sin as a potential underlying problem to difficulties that believers face in their lives. All difficulties are, of course, the direct or indirect consequence of sin being in the world, but not necessarily the sin of individual concerned. Moving towards the resolution of the emotional or behavioural problem must involve dealing with such sin, where it has occurred, as that is a condition of receiving the Lord's blessing. Where there is un-confessed sin, God must necessarily deal with us in discipline (Heb.12:4-11). It is an important role of the counselor to help in the identification and acknowledgement of such sin. It may also involve providing instruction on the path of repentance and recovery.

The Need for Repentance and Confession

The only and proper remedy for sin is repentance and confession, relying on the sure promise of 1 John 1:9 for forgiveness and cleansing: *"If we confess our sins, He is faithful and righteous to forgive us our sins and to cleanse us from all unrighteousness."*

Confession essentially means agreement - coming into full agreement with God about what we've done. It should always of course be accompanied by forsaking the sin. If the sin is addictive, this may require on-going assistance. It is doing no favour to a person to disguise sin as a sickness or genetic disposition. Repentance (a true change of mind and attitude to the behaviour) is something that only God can give (2 Tim.2:25).

The Evidence of Repentance

The evidence of repentance would normally include seeing the person:

    a. showing an attitude of true humility, contrition and remorse towards God (and not just shame in other peoples' eyes);

    b. expressing an understanding of the wrong, its seriousness and the damage done;

    c. not repeating the sin;

    d. showing willingness to get appropriate help in cases of chronic weakness or addiction;

    e. being willing to confess the sin to God in the presence of overseers, and to any others affected; and

    f. being willing to make amends (to the extent possible) and to accept any inevitable consequences of the wrongdoing (Gal.6:7,8) including any legal penalties.

A simple statement to the effect that "God has forgiven me" is usually far from sufficient.

> *"He who covers his sins will not prosper, but whoever confesses and forsakes them will have mercy"* (Prov.28:13).

We need to realize that we are never going to be without problems and challenges in this life, and we are never going to become sinless *("If we say that we have no sin, we deceive ourselves, and the truth is not in us" -* 1 Jn.1:8*)*. But sin needs to be promptly recognized and cleared up, or it will hamper any future progress.

17. THE SKILLS OF COUNSELING

"Let every man be swift to hear, slow to speak" (Jas.1:19).

Among the conversational skills required by a good counselor, three are particularly important: asking questions, listening effectively and confronting. The first two are essential in conducting what is in effect an interview. Confronting is required at some stage in order to challenge the person regarding their thinking and consequent behaviour. Without the first two, it is virtually impossible to arrive at a proper understanding of the underlying problem; without the third, no change can be expected to result from the encounter.

A. The Skill of Questioning

As we see in the case of the Lord Jesus on the road to Emmaus (see chapter 22), He began and continued the conversation by asking questions and listening to their answers. Asking good questions, and asking them in an effective way, is essential to helping a person open up and divulge the particulars of the problem they are facing. It is also the means by which the truth of the situation, at the necessary depth of understanding, can be discovered. By directing the conversation by asking purposeful questions, a great deal of direction and insight can be provided. It can result in the person articulating problems and views that they had never expressed before.

Properly framed and sequenced questions, which elicit meaningful responses, can be a powerful tool in enabling someone to discover truth for themselves without having to directly tell them. Questions tend to be less threatening than just telling or giving advice, which can be perceived as lecturing. A good interview combines the power of questioning with "empathetic" listening. A good interviewer generally does less than half the talking in the counseling conversation.

Following are some general guidelines for counselors to use to ask good questions in a counseling situation:

Do...

- Ask probing questions rather than stopping when you have received general answers. Often the initial answer can be quite superficial, which is not sufficient to diagnose the real issue. Ask for specifics, such as: "Can you give me an example of that?"; and "What do you mean by that?" "How does that relate to what you said about ...?"
- Be conversational in style. It is not an interrogation. Insert occasional comments, give reactions, and pause periodically. Let subsequent questions flow from previous answers.
- Ask "what" questions in order to get facts. Seek clarification of the problem.
- Control where the conversation is going. The person may ramble, but the counselor must know where to steer the interview.

Don't

- Don't ask yes/no questions, except to confirm some information (or later to confirm a commitment to action). Rather, ask questions that require some elaboration.
- Don't ask questions where the answer is implicit, or "lead the witness"; it isn't a court of law. Examples might be: "Isn't it true that ..."; "Doesn't it seem that ...".
- Don't ramble; people tend to respond to the last sentence they hear.
- Don't dwell unnecessarily on the problem and so encourage morbid introspection or groveling. When sufficient information has been obtained, move on to the solution

phase.

- Don't confuse the person with their wrong behaviour. The wrong behaviour should not be condoned, but the person themselves should be unconditionally accepted.
- Don't talk about yourself, other than briefly to the extent appropriate in order to establish rapport. Changing the subject from them to you is a real inhibitor to them opening up.
- Don't be threatening or jump to conclusions.

B) The Skill of Listening

Listening to someone may sound like an easy thing to do, because we hear people speak to us all the time. But listening in such a way that their true meaning registers with us with regard to deep personal issues in their lives is not so automatic. What is needed by a good counselor is active and attentive listening that encourages the speaker to express themselves openly. Without it, good counseling conversations cannot occur. Listening with empathy (that is, listening for the meaning of what is being said) requires discipline. It also shows that the counselor cares.

Some common obstacles to this type of listening include:

- Being concerned about what to say next, after the other person is finished speaking. This distracts attention away from what is being said. It is far more effective to give total concentration, and then pause if necessary before responding. It is a sign of respect to show that you are thinking seriously about how to respond to what they have just said.
- Body language that indicates less than full interest, such as looking or turning away, frowning, folding your arms and leaning back, and stiffness. The person should have your total

attention, although you should not just stare.

- Interrupting when the person is speaking. This is a major deterrent to their openness, as it indicates that you think that what you have to say is more important than what they have to say.

- A useful method of showing attentiveness, and of obtaining clarification, is to paraphrase briefly what the person has just been saying, and to ask them if you have understood them properly. This is a helpful means of feedback to ensure that the message that was intended to be conveyed (and not just the words) was in fact received.

- Positive affirmations such as nodding, agreeing, and smiling can encourage the person to continue, especially if what they are saying is somewhat painful, since it indicates that you are not being judgmental.

- In some cases, it may be advisable for the counselor to take notes to retain a lot of pertinent information, but this should only be done with the person's prior permission. Of course, assurance as to the complete privacy and restricted use of the notes must be given.

Some other suggestions for good listening in counseling situations include:

- Empathize with suffering, but do not indulge excessive self-pity. Scriptures exhort Christians to trust and obey the Lord even when suffering (1 Pet.4:19).

- Don't jump to conclusions. The first answer given may not be the real problem or the whole problem. It usually requires some probing to establish the real underlying issues.

- Do not allow another person to be criticized in their absence. The counselor should always bring the person back to their own actions, feelings and thinking, and not allow the blaming of others to distract from this.

- Do not generalize the problem or offer "pat" answers. Each person and their situation is unique in some respect and requires the care and the courtesy of being addresses individually.

C) The Skill of Confronting

At some point in the counseling process, the counselor must stop just asking questions; they have to begin to challenge the person about their beliefs, assumptions and behaviour. This is where the true counseling starts to takes place. Everything that precedes it is diagnostic, hopefully resulting in the person understanding adequately and accepting the cause of their difficulty. But confrontation of some type is needed in order to bring about change. The confrontation must be done firmly but lovingly - "*speaking the truth in love*" (Eph.4:15).

The purpose of confrontation is to help the person see things differently. Essentially it involves them coming to view their situation as God Himself sees it, as shown in the scriptures. They then need to be challenged to put that into practice, to bring their actions into line with God's Word. This requires faith in the real sense - an implicit trust that what God says about their situation is in fact the truth, as opposed to the way they had been thinking. It is one thing to get a committed disciple of the Lord Jesus to agree mentally with the scriptural point of view, but quite another to get them to relinquish their own behaviour and adopt new behaviour based on it. People generally do not change ingrained beliefs easily, even when faced with clear and explicit words of scripture. They are often fairly adept at rationalizing the divergence.

During a counseling conversation it may be appropriate to challenge an answer that the person has given. Some examples include:

- Where they are evading an issue or making excuses;

- To help them to face reality and be completely honest;
- To help them to broaden their perspective on the problem;
- To show them that they are responsible for the consequences of their own behaviour;
- To convince them that they can in fact take appropriate steps to address their difficulty, and that they are not the victim of someone else's past or present behaviour;
- To help them to recognize unhealthy behaviour, such as punishing themselves;
- When there are inconsistencies between what they say and what they do (which may occur if they are just trying to give answers to please the counselor);
- If they are being too vague about actions they are willing to undertake;
- If they resist hearing the truth from the counselor.

It is essential for the counselor to be sure of their facts before confronting the person, as there may well be resistance. Confrontation can never challenge them as a person, but just their actions and their thinking. It must always be done non-judgmentally, in love and acceptance. In fact, the stronger the confrontation, the greater level of support is required of the counselor. This is our next topic.

"... with all lowliness and gentleness, with longsuffering, bearing with one another in love" (Eph.4:2).

The good counselor does more than provide good advice and instruction. He or she acts as a spiritual mentor throughout the process, showing by example how to rely on the Lord for the answers to life's difficulties. Counsel and exhortation needs to be accompanied by intercessory prayer on behalf of the individual. In addition, to the extent the person being helped is willing at each stage, the counselor may pray with them.

Being Supportive

The early stage of a counseling intervention is designed primarily to diagnose the underlying problem. However it should also serve another vital purpose - to build rapport in preparation for the later stage where it will be necessary to challenge the person's behaviour and thinking. Support for the individual and in their attempts to face their difficulties must be constant and apparent.

If the person senses that they are being judged or punished, or that the counselor is disinterested, they will stop actively participating. Support is especially important when the counselor confronts wrong beliefs or behaviour. Support is evidenced by taking the full time that is required, paying full attention, positive body language, good tone of voice, sensitive framing of questions, and talking less than half the time (but acknowledging and providing feedback). It is necessary to be honest, open and obviously fair. Establish rapport in order to communicate true acceptance and so encourage risk-taking for making changes. The person should feel that they and the counselor are a team solving the problem together.

Some dangers to avoid in this respect are:

- Probing just to satisfy your own curiosity;
- Acting antagonistically or superior;
- Making decisions for the person, or taking responsibility for their actions;
- Being too talkative, rambling or using generalities;
- Talking too much about your own experiences;
- Becoming personally involved (which results in loss of objectivity);
- Being drawn into partaking of the sin (Gal.6:1);
- Betraying confidences;
- Being just theoretical and impractical;
- Being in too much of a hurry;

- Jumping to conclusions; and
- Telling them 'what' to do but not 'how' to do it.

18. HOW TO RESOLVE CONFLICT

"Be at peace among yourselves" (1 Thess.5:13).

Often the problems that require counseling assistance do not just involve one individual. They often involve two or more people who are in a relationship, such as marriage partners, members of a family, or two saints in an assembly. Often the intervention of a third-party counselor is requested, by one or both of the protagonists, or else by another person who is concerned about the situation. The third party needs to be credible to both sides and needs the permission of both to become involved. Use of a suitable and objective third party can often help to clarify and resolve the issues, and to help both people understand the other's point of view. It can help to ensure that a productive process is followed and is not defeated by emotional reactions of the parties involved in the course of what may be difficult confrontation.

Relationship Counseling

Where counseling takes place with both people present, both of them must be willing to engage in the process in the expectation that it will help them find a solution. If either party is unwilling, or is there only by coercion, the process is not likely to be successful. A barrier to reconciliation is if one or both of them are primarily determined to prove they are right and justify themselves, rather than to mend the relationship. If the counselor detects any reluctance, it needs to be addressed explicitly, such as buy asking "Why did you come here to see me?". The consequences of not resolving the problem may need to be made explicit to the parties in order to show them that it is worth the effort to persevere.

Communication Problems

Many relationship problems are primarily communication problems - the two parties have different perceptions of the same facts. This may happen where the particular issue that caused the problem is not overly significant, but it has been blown out of proportion by misunderstanding of what actually happened or what was said, and what the motives behind it were. There may be a lack of two-way communication because one of them has "shut off" and won't talk about it, or else because the meaning is not getting through.

In this latter case an "echo" process can help. This involves asking the first person to speak and then asking the second person: "What did you just hear him/her say?". Then ask the first person; "Is that what you meant?". This can be useful in revealing misunderstandings. Another technique is "reverse role play", where each person earnestly argues the other's point of view.

Fear

Some inter-personal problems can be caused by fear, such as fear of rejection or failure. This can result in unproductive emotional patterns of relating to the other person. Examples of this are:

- always saying what you think the other person wants to hear (being a "pleaser");
- not engaging in discussing the issues (to avoid unpleasant consequences, or due to feeling unable to hold up their end of the discussion);
- undermining the other person's efforts, by putting them down;
- changing the subject to an issue they can win at;
- hiding behind judgments of people ("labels") - such as "Well you know he always exaggerates";
- being stubborn ("my way or the highway"); and
- verbally attacking the other person.

In these cases the counselor can ask the question: "What is it that you are you afraid of? If the problem is that the person always has to be "right", they probably learned at some stage that it's not OK to be wrong. They may have been punished for that in their childhood.

Manipulative Behaviour

Sometimes a person will have been withholding affection and acceptance from another person in an attempt to motivate certain behaviour or performance by them. For example they may go quiet or sullen in an attempt to get permission to do something. This approach usually backfires, and they need to be shown that this is the case. Each person needs to be able to say to the other one what they need and want from them in very specific terms. When one person says positive things about the other, ask the other "How does that sound when you hear it?".

Sin Against Each Other

Any sinful behaviour needs to be confessed to the other person, in a true attitude of repentance and contrition. The other person then needs to be urged to forgive, on the basis of scripture. They need to realize that forgiveness is a choice, not a feeling.

> "... forgiving one another, just as God in Christ forgave you" (Eph.4:32).

Often in interventions of this kind there is value in one or both of the people communicating with the other in writing, by sending them a letter. A letter is more formal than a telephone conversation or eMail and tends to be taken more seriously. It allows the writer to say a lot more without interruption, and it can serve as a point of reference in future. It needs to be written with great care, both as to content and tone, and with regard to the possibility it may be seen by someone else.

Mediation – an Approach

Conflict resolution involves addressing both the underlying issues and the relationship itself. The purpose is to close the gap between them and, by helping the participants to deal with the issues that have created the conflict, to mend the relationship. The counselor becomes a mediator to draw the two people together. A mediator is different in this respect from a negotiator or an arbitrator.

Depending on how far apart the relationship presently is, the two people may or may not be willing to meet with a counselor together initially. If not, the counselor should meet with each separately. The objective, however, is to reach the point where they are willing to meet together with the counselor to resolve the problem. Usually each person will only do this if they have heard and believe that the other person:

(a) wants the relationship to be mended;

(b) is willing to acknowledge their own part in the problem; and

(c) will be willing to forgive them for their part in it.

Generally the overall process involves three stages.

A) Information Gathering

Having received permission, the counselor would meet with each person separately to ascertain their version of the facts, their understanding of the wrongs done on both sides, and their attitude towards reconciliation. On the basis of the principle "seek first to understand before seeking to be understood", the first meeting may simply be for information gathering through interviewing and listening. Sometimes it is useful to make notes (after asking permission), to avoid having to rely on memory later. It also gives credence to the things being said.

Often in these cases there is a communication problem between the parties. Either no information is flowing between them, so that they are unaware of certain things, or it is so distorted and misinterpreted that it is counter-productive. Where there is a relationship problem, each party will tend to interpret any information about the other through their own emotional perspective, which increases the potential for misunderstanding.

Having had information-gathering conversations with both parties, the counselor should be able afterwards on their own to reflect on what was said and begin to make sense out of it. They should identify agreements and disagreements on facts. They should also be able to see where either or both persons have gone astray (which they may have attempted to justify) and how the other person has interpreted that. If necessary, they may need to again meet with the parties individually, to clarify facts and fill in blanks.

B) Negotiating a Joint Meeting

This second step involves again meeting with the two parties separately to review areas of agreement and disagreement between the two reports, and to ascertain their willingness to try to overcome the problem. Misperceptions due to communication difficulties can be addressed out, and hope and optimism of a successful outcome can be expressed. Each person needs to be helped to see the situation through the other person's eyes. They should be asked "What do you want and need from them", and "What would like to say to them?".

It is vital throughout this whole process that neither person perceives a bias in the counselor, or that we are acting as an advocate for one side or the other. They must at all times be open, honest and obviously fair. The focus must be on future action, while fully acknowledging the past and present.

It may be possible at this stage to get each side to agree to forgive the other if the other will forgive them – a kind of dual conditional forgiveness. Sometimes just the emotional release of having been able to express their point of view to a responsive listener will be enough. However, many times it will not be. But if this point is reached, a mutual meeting is possible.

If one or both persons is unwilling to meet to forgive and reconcile, more work needs to be done with them individually to discover if there are further hidden causes, and to discuss the impact of a lack of a resolution, and payoffs to resolution for each. This is more in the nature of individual counseling (as discussed in previous chapters).

Sometimes a useful step at this point can be to have the two parties write a personal letter to each other, if they agree to do so. The letter can state their version of what happened and how they feel about it, and can express a willingness to forgive and be reconciled. A letter has the advantage of allowing more complete expression of thoughts, expressed with the right tone, and will usually be read completely without interruption, unlike much face-to-face communications. It also avoids the risk of negative body language confusing what is being said. Such letters can often pave the way for a meeting.

C) Facilitating the Joint Meeting

Once both parties have agreed to meet together with the counselor, the counselor should arrange a mutually convenient time and place, on neutral ground. Since the introductions will likely be awkward, the counselor should normally take control of the meeting at the start and keep the small talk to a minimum. Reading a suitable scripture and praying first can help set the tone, but it is usually better without comment, which could be interpreted as preaching or bias.

The counselor should state that both sides have agreed to the meeting, summarize the points of agreement reached in the individual meetings, identify the wrongs that each party has said they were willing to admit to, state that both sides had said they were willing to forgive the other, and then invite one of them to initiate the conversation. The counselor should not include anything that had not previously been covered with both parties individually. There should be no surprises, as it could indicate a breach of trust. If the conversation between the two persons takes a direction towards just rehashing the problem or recriminations, the counselor needs to intervene to restate the purpose of the meeting. If things are going well, however, the counselor can sit back and listen and let things take their course.

These types of meetings can be quite emotional, which is quite acceptable. The counselor can affirm that it is quite OK to cry, for example. But the meeting needs to conclude with each party agreeing to specific positive actions they will take towards each other in the near future, and for which they can be held accountable. There may also be the need to deal with fallout of the problem – effects on other people ("collateral damage"), and derivative sins by others such as gossip, false accusations or taking sides. Once the parties themselves have reconciled, they can help to quash these peripheral disturbances. Finally, the counselor should schedule a follow-up with them, which should be agreed to by both.

"Blessed are the peacemakers, for they shall be called sons of God" (Matt.5:9).

Resolving Conflicts in the Church

The above guidance is especially applicable to married couples or potentially even family members. However, the following two scriptures provide the proper way for two disciples who are in conflict to deal with it. The first deals with the situation where a brother or sister has been offended, and the second with where someone is offended at them, but in both cases the key is not to let the matter fester but deal with it:

> *"If your brother sins against you, go and tell him his fault between you and him alone. If he hears you, you have gained your brother. But if he will not hear, take with you one or two more, that 'by the mouth of two or three witnesses every word may be established.' And if he refuses to hear them, tell it to the church. But if he refuses even to hear the church, let him be to you like a heathen and a tax collector"* (Matt.18:15-17).

> *"If you bring your gift to the altar, and there remember that your brother has something against you, leave your gift there before the altar, and go your way. First be reconciled to your brother, and then come and offer your gift"* (Matt.5:23-24).

19. HOW TO HELP IN A CRISIS

"Many are the afflictions of the righteous, But the Lord delivers him out of them all" (Ps.34:19).

Life is full of its ups and downs and we all develop our own ways of responding and dealing with them – our "coping mechanisms". But occasionally things happen that really upset our equilibrium, and which we cannot resolve in the usual way. We refer to these as crises. They are critical circumstances where the outcome is uncertain, and yet it matters a great deal to us. When they occur, they tend to be all-absorbing.

Two Types of Crises

Crises can be of two general types. One is the emergency – the sudden, urgent situation where there is danger, and something needs to be done quickly. Examples include:

- a serious car accident;
- a fire in the home; a lost child; or
- a heart attack.

The other type is not urgent, but it involves a serious threat. Examples include:

- diagnosis of a fatal illness;
- threatened or actual marriage breakup;
- unwanted (and perhaps illegitimate) pregnancy;
- death of a loved one;
- financial disaster; and
- major life changes – for example, we use the term "mid-life crisis" to describe one type of major adjustment in life.

The Bible gives many examples of people experiencing crises in their lives – such as Job's sudden loss of family and possessions and his affliction. Abraham had several - the upheaval of his home when he was called to leave Ur, Sarah's childlessness, and God's command to offer their son Isaac. The apostle Paul cited many perils in his life in 2 Corinthians 11:26. And so crises are to be expected. How does God expect us to deal with them? And does He give us the means to do so?

Emotional Reactions to Crises

Emotional reactions to crises can be very strong and debilitating. They can cover the whole gamut of:

- guilt (if we feel responsible for causing the crisis);
- anger (if we feel it's unfair);
- anxiety (because we don't know what the outcome is going to be);
- inadequacy (if we feel helpless in the situation); and
- depression (if we feel the situation is hopeless).

If the situation is urgent, anxiety and fear can be an especially strong emotion. High levels of anxiety have major impacts. They can:

- immobilize us;
- impair our performance;
- shorten our concentration span,
- block our memory;
- block our ability to communicate; and
- cause physical symptoms such as intense headaches and paralysis.

It is for this reason that someone else can be of great assistance to a person going through a crisis.

Scriptural Cases

There are two particularly instructive cases of crises in the Bible, both of which were storms at sea. The first involved the Lord and His disciples on the Sea of Galilee:

> *"On the same day, when evening had come, He said to them, "Let us cross over to the other side." Now when they had left the multitude, they took Him along in the boat as He was. And other little boats were also with Him. And a great windstorm arose, and the waves beat into the boat, so that it was already filling. But He was in the stern, asleep on a pillow. And they awoke Him and said to Him, "Teacher, do You not care that we are perishing?" Then He arose and rebuked the wind, and said to the sea, "Peace, be still!" And the wind ceased and there was a great calm. But He said to them, "Why are you so fearful? How is it that you have no faith?" And they feared exceedingly, and said to one another, "Who can this be, that even the wind and the sea obey Him!"* (Mk.4:35-41).

Here was a case where the disciples, who were experienced fishermen, were terrified by the storm. Luke 8:23 says they were in jeopardy. But Jesus wasn't panicking; He never did. He was always in control, no matter the situation. He was asleep in the boat. When they aroused Him, He first calmed their fears, and then calmed the cause of their fears - the storm. The end result of the crisis was that they had a greater appreciation of Him - "what kind of person is this!". One of those disciples who was panicking was Peter. What a contrast a few years later when he was in prison, waiting to be executed the next day, and yet he was sound asleep when the angel came to rescue him (Acts 12:6).

The second storm was when Paul was being taken prisoner to Rome. Here are some excerpts from the account:

"A tempestuous head wind arose, called Euroclydon. So when the ship was caught, and could not head into the wind, we let her drive ... they used cables to under-gird the ship; and fearing lest they should run aground ... we were exceedingly tempest-tossed ... Now when neither sun nor stars appeared for many days, and no small tempest beat on us, all hope that we would be saved was finally given up. But after long abstinence from food, then Paul stood in the midst of them and said, "Men, you should have listened to me, and not have sailed from Crete and incurred this disaster and loss. And now I urge you to take heart, for there will be no loss of life among you, but only of the ship.

For there stood by me this night an angel of the God to whom I belong and whom I serve, saying, 'Do not be afraid, Paul; you must be brought before Caesar; and indeed God has granted you all those who sail with you.' "Therefore take heart, men, for I believe God that it will be just as it was told me ... Now when the fourteenth night had come... as the sailors were seeking to escape from the ship ... Paul said to the centurion and the soldiers, "Unless these men stay in the ship, you cannot be saved ... And as day was about to dawn, Paul implored them all to take food, saying, "Today is the fourteenth day you have waited and continued without food, and eaten nothing. Therefore I urge you to take nourishment, for this is for your survival, since not a hair will fall from the head of any of you." And when he had said these things, he took bread and gave thanks to God in the presence of them all; and when he had broken it he began to eat. Then they were all encouraged, and also took food themselves. And in all we were two hundred and seventy-six persons on the ship ... so it was that they all escaped safely to land" (Acts 27:13-44).

Despite being a prisoner and not having eaten for two weeks, Paul took charge in this crisis. His calmness in what must have been a chaotic situation, and His evident and explicit trust in God, were an encouragement to the others on board. Rank and status no longer mattered in the situation; they were all human beings just trying to survive. He told them what they had to do and they responded, and took courage. And all 276 of them survived.

Being Useful in a Crisis

God has supplied us as disciples of Christ with the means to deal with the various crises that can beset us. Often He uses others to come along side to apply His gifts in assisting in a crisis. 1 Corinthians 12:28 refers to the gifts of "helps". Ironically, it is the same word that is used (in the King James Version) in Acts 27:17 for the cables that under-girded the ship that Paul was on. They prevented the ship from going to pieces. Meanwhile, on board, Paul was using the gift of "helps" to prevent the passengers from "going to pieces". The gift of helps was also seen in the Old Testament when the seventy elders were given to Moses to assist him in bearing the peoples' burdens (Num.11:17).

There are several gifts that apply in times of crises, and we as individuals don't necessarily have to be "specially gifted" in order to use them. The Bible itemizes many spiritual gifts; Romans 12:6-8 identifies seven; 1 Corinthians 12:8-10 identifies nine, and verse 28 identifies five more. 1 Corinthians 13 ends by listing three "abiding" gifts (faith, hope and love) and classes love as the greatest of them. Of all these the following outlines how six gifts in particular can be applied to help someone in a crisis situation. They are shown as six "steps", although they don't always happen in strict sequence.

Step 1 – Make Contact

Sometimes people ask for help in a crisis, but often they don't due to confusion, embarrassment, uncertainty, pride, and busyness. If the Lord puts a burden on our heart when we hear of someone facing a crisis situation, we should act on it and make contact. We should go to them if we can; if we can't, we should phone them. Even if it turns out we can't help or aren't wanted, we need to take the chance and go. (It is worth the risk of being rejected.)

Rule number one is "show up". Even though we may not have the remedy or the answers, the show of support will usually be very helpful and will be appreciated. It is the gift of love in action. It was the love showed by the Lord to His disciples on several occasions when they were so disturbed after His death. For example, He went especially to Peter, then to the two on the way to Emmaus, then to the upper room, and then to Thomas. It was the love He showed in going to Martha and Mary when their brother had died. It was the love the good Samaritan showed to the wounded man (in Lk.10:34 it says that he *"went to him"*). We go in order to fulfill 1 Thessalonians 5:11: *"Therefore comfort each other and edify one another, just as you also are doing."*. People do not easily forget such acts of kindness in times of need.

Even in extreme cases, such as suicide threats, where there may be reluctance to become involved, research has shown that a trusted friend can be more helpful than a professional counselor. We can, in effect, be the presence of Christ to another person, just as the Lord was there in the boat in the storm. Him being there made all the difference. Depending on the situation, we need to be prepared to stay with the person as long as necessary. This may well be inconvenient to us, but it may be very helpful to the person in the crisis.

"Love suffers long and is kind" (1 Cor.13:4).

Step 2 – Reduce Anxiety

Anxiety is contagious, but so is calmness. The presence of a calm, caring person can be reassuring to someone in crisis and can help them to think through and then do what is needed. It is the gift of peace. *("Blessed are the peacemakers"* – Matt.5:9). Peace in the Bible not only refers to peace from conflict, which is often called "rest", but also peace of mind.

Frequently in scripture, when the Lord (or an angel) appeared to people, they were afraid. The first thing they were usually told was *"don't be afraid"*. Quelling the fear is a first priority if responsible action is to be taken. The disciples in the boat must have wondered where Christ always got His calmness from. He never got rattled, and there were many occasions where He could have been. Then in the upper room He talked to them about His impending death. They were confused and upset, but He wasn't. The only times He got angry was because of concern for others – such as His anger at the money-changers who were desecrating His Father's house, and at the disciples who held back the children from Him. His soul was troubled as He anticipated Calvary (Jn.12:27), but it wasn't a feeling of anxiety or helplessness. Peter tried to deny the reality of Christ's upcoming death (Matt.16:22), but denial is no cure for anxiety. Where did Christ's serenity come from? How could He always be in control? And so in the upper room He gave them the answer:

> *"Peace I leave with you, My peace I give to you; not as the world gives do I give to you"* (Jn.14:27).

His peace came from a different place, a divine source, and He gave it to them (and to us - it is the third description of the fruit of the Holy Spirit in our lives – *"love, joy, peace ..."*). It has a different source than the world's way of handling anxiety; it is based on the sure knowledge that God is always in control. That is the cause of our peace. God never has a crisis. And we can be peacemakers to other people. Calmness is a great gift to give. We can be the means to help people access that divine source of peace, when panic may be the instinctive response.

"God is our refuge and strength, a very present help in trouble. Therefore we will not fear ..." (Ps.46:1,2).

"We know that all things work together for good to those who love God, to those who are the called according to His purpose" (Rom.8:28).

Step 3 – Focus on What's Important

Confusion and anxiety in a crisis can lead to paralysis – the person just doesn't know what to do, and so does nothing. They may get lots of conflicting advice (as Job did from his friends), but this just adds to the confusion and the pressure of the situation. What is needed is gentle leadership, taking charge with permission. (A leader is someone who: (1) knows what needs to be done; (2) takes initiative; and (3) gets the support of others.) Leadership in such a situation to provide clarity of thinking is a gift from God (Rom.12:8).

Leading is not bossing the person around or ignoring their wishes. That just adds to the crisis. Don't become part of the problem. The KJV uses the word "rule" for leadership but to us today that has an authoritarian ring to it, which is not what is meant. A good rule of thumb is "Do what they can't do for themselves – but not any more". If they are able to participate, get their agreement on what needs to be done.

Exercizing leadership for someone in a crisis helps them to:

(1) think clearly and objectively;

(2) do the most important things first (such as: save a life, avoid serious injury); and

(3) avoid destructive actions (such as looking for revenge) instead of solving the real problem.

It can also help the person to accept the reality of the situation, as our minds often protect us by causing us to think the situation is not really happening. Personal support is very helpful in achieving this acceptance of reality.

It is important not to minimize what the person is going through. If it's important to them, then we need to treat it as just as important. Being dismissive of someone's concern can be very hurtful. We should also avoid making them feel worse by talking about their blame for the crisis (which is what Job's friends did to him). We also should avoid giving empty assurances that "everything's going to be all right" if we don't know that to be true.

"He leads me beside the still waters" (Ps.23:2).

Step 4 – Assess the Resources

Often help is needed in a crisis to deal with specific problems. It may require specialized expertise, such as a doctor, a police officer, an insurance agent, or a lawyer. It may require quick access to money, or the need to contact family members, or to ask others to pray. What are needed are the twin gifts of knowledge and wisdom (1 Cor.12:8). Knowledge is having the pertinent information; wisdom is having the skill to apply it in the particular situation. Knowledge can consist of such practical things as: the location of the nearest hospital; what to do in the event of a car accident; what agencies are available to help with particular problems; and key phone numbers. Skill can include life-saving techniques, negotiation techniques, and self-defense.

While the gifts of knowledge and wisdom are God-given, they are not miraculous in nature. We don't just receive them passively. They have to be acquired and developed. An example of this is the fine workmanship that was used in making the furniture for the tabernacle in the wilderness, by Bezalel, Aholiab and other gifted artisans. The Lord said: *"I have filled him with the Spirit of God, in wisdom, in understanding, in knowledge, and in all manner of workmanship, to design artistic works, to work in gold, in silver, in bronze, in cutting jewels for setting, in carving wood, and to work in all manner of workmanship"* (Ex.31:3-5). While God gifted these people with knowledge and wisdom for the work, it is almost certain that they had learned this craft previously in Egypt. Preparation and development of skill is essential. The gift is, in effect, the ability to acquire the knowledge and the skill.

Prayer is of course an indispensable resource in a crisis, even if brief, silent prayers are all that are possible. But it accesses the power of God on our behalf, and reminds us of whom we are relying on in the situation. Praying (and then thanking) in very specific terms increases our sense of the presence of God. If we are praying for wisdom from God in the circumstances (as Jas.1:5 instructs us about), we should expect to receive it. When it comes we should recognize it as coming from God (James gives its characteristics in 3:17). One of the ways to help in the situation is to mobilize the prayers of others, such as was done in Jerusalem when Peter was imprisoned (Acts 12:5).

Just as with compulsory lifeboat drills and fire drills, we can prepare for emergencies to some extent. Carrying relevant phone numbers, rehearsing "what if" scenarios, having tools and equipment on hand (such as a cell phone), instructing children at home, etc. are all examples.

Step 5 – Plan and Take Action

It takes faith and courage to act in a crisis, and a helper can stimulate this. It is the gift of exhortation (Rom.12:8). "Exhorting" in scripture is almost always related to taking specific action, not just giving encouragement to feel better. When the disciples were faced with five thousand hungry people, the Lord told them to: (a) take inventory of the food they had; and (b) organize the people into manageable groups.

Often quick decisions need to be made, and alternative actions evaluated. The helper needs to have a bias to action, not discussion, without forcing his or her will. Even if not a lot can be done, doing something creates a sense of some momentum, which can generate hopefulness, as Paul's actions on the boat in Acts 27 demonstrate. In the case of Lazarus' death, after the Lord had heard Martha and Mary express how they were feeling, he took action by asking them to show Him where Lazarus' grave was (even though He already knew).

Step 6 – Instill Hope

Having realistic hope is necessary in a crisis situation. It brings relief from suffering ("things will get better"), avoids despair, and releases energy to deal with the situation. Thinking on the positive aspects, rather than dwelling on the negative, which is a very natural thing to do, is important for taking constructive action. (Scientific studies on cases of illness, school grades and prisoners, for example, show that hope is a strong predictor of outcomes.) Hope is more than just wishing. A helper can play an important part in providing reassurance about the outcome in a crisis.

Three ways a helper can instill hope are:

(1) referring to, or reminding the person of, key applicable truths and promises of God in scripture and expressing faith in them (while avoiding them sounding like clichés;

(2) challenging any self-defeating thinking (such as: "I couldn't do that"; or "Why does this always happen to me?"); and

(3) get them moving and doing something, to show that they aren't helpless (such as: "Why don't you see if your passenger is all right, and I'll phone for the police").

"... we were saved in this hope, but hope that is seen is not hope" (Rom.8:24).

"We are hard pressed on every side, yet not crushed; we are perplexed, but not in despair; persecuted, but not forsaken; struck down, but not destroyed." (2 Cor.4:7-9).

Summary

For ease of remembering, these steps can all be named with words that start with the letter "C", and they all use a gift from God. They are His provision to enable us to help someone get through a crisis:

- Contact (the gift of love);
- Calmness (the gift of peace);
- Clarity (the gift of leadership);
- Competence (the gifts of knowledge and wisdom);
- Courage (the gift of exhortation); and
- Confidence (the gift of hope).

It may well be that the eventual outcome of the crisis will be a deepened sense of the care and provision of the Lord for all involved. This will be something that they and we can later share with others as the story is told (as it will be).

20. MARITAL COUNSELING

"Heirs together of the grace of life" (1 Pet.3:7).

Giving counsel to couples who are preparing to marry, or to couples that are already married, is a particular type of counseling situation because of the intimacy and intended permanence of the relationship. Where such counseling is provided, it is usually best done by another married couple, and one that is experienced and godly in their own relationship. Many Christian couples may be reluctant to offer this type of assistance because they are aware of imperfections in their own marriage, and they may well have experienced some rocky times together. But, provided that their present marriage relationship is fundamentally sound and is based on a solid and Biblical relationship with the Lord, they can be of great help to others.

Following are a number of issues that can be very useful to help couples to discuss with each other.

Oneness in Marriage

Maintaining "oneness" is the critical issue in marriage. Husbands and wives generally are very different; God made us that way. Oneness does not mean eliminating our differences or becoming alike. We are "opposite sexes"; our differences are substantial and permanent. However, the union of a man and a woman in marriage generates the power to love (while division between them creates the power to hurt each other). Some things that can threaten this oneness in a marriage include:

Not Making the Difficult Adjustments Required

Our culture and lifestyle today imposes difficulties, such as altered husbands' and wives' roles, changing morals, and increasing disregard for authority. Where we as a couple have contrasting backgrounds (such as our values, education, vocations, religion, finances, blended families) it makes adjustments necessary by each of us. If there are superficial motivations for the marriage (feelings, sexual attraction, cultural pressures, an escape) these can create real problems, as can differing expectations by the man and woman (of their spouse's responsibilities, how to express love, and sexual performance).

Trying to Follow the World's Plan

The world's plan for a successful marriage is 50:50 performance ("You do your part, and I'll do mine"). However, it is doomed to failure. Both people tend to think that they're doing the giving. The 50% can't be measured. We are unable to meet unreal and unknown expectations. We can tend to focus on our mate's weaknesses, not their strengths. Disappointment in our mate paralyzes our own performance. The 50:50 plan results in the present success rate for marriages in the world - 50:50 (a 50% divorce rate).

Natural Selfishness

Our society's culture promotes independence and self-centredness ("looking out for number one"). During dating, we don't normally see the real person. Selfishness causes us to reject the other person; we think our mate is the problem when it's really our self-centredness.

Trials and Difficulties

We need to (a) anticipate the inevitability of trials; and (b) respond properly to them when they occur. God allows them for a reason; they are an opportunity for growth. The fact that difficulties occur do not by themselves indicate that the marriage is in trouble. We may tend to suppress the problems or try to escape from them. We need to realize that our mate is not our enemy, and that we need to work through the difficulties together.

Extra-marital Affairs

Extramarital affairs are actually attempts to escape from reality and find fulfillment outside the marriage. There are many types of affairs. They can be (a) love affairs; (b) career affairs; (c) materialism affairs; or (d) activities affairs. They all involve substituting something in place of the marriage relationship and what it should provide. It therefore deprives our partner of some attention, affection (and perhaps financial support). Someone has said that "The world's formula for success is the same as for a nervous breakdown".

We can develop a wrong perception of reality in our life, which the world tends to feed (e.g. by sexual or materialistic advertising). We then contrast that illusion with our own situation and become unrealistically dissatisfied. This can lead to escapism, first in our minds and then perhaps in action. But escapism ends in isolation, the very opposite to oneness.

God's Purposes for Oneness

People marry primarily to achieve togetherness, companionship and love. It was God's idea. It was the first institution in society, the first system of interdependent relationships. It is the priority relationship in a family and gives stability to children. God designed it to be a lifetime commitment between one man and one woman (not between two men or two women, and not between multiple partners). God gave Adam a woman, not another man. Oneness needs to be experienced (a) vertically, with God, and (b) horizontally, with each other, in a triangular relationship, like the godhead itself.

God's purposes for us in marriage include:

- Mirroring God's image on earth (Gen.1:26,27). A man and a wife are made to be different, so that together they can mirror

God's image. A failed marriage affects God's reputation in the eyes of others.

- Mutually completing each other (Gen.2:18; 1 Cor.11:11). The companionship replaces the isolation and loneliness. It takes time and sacrifice to work out differences, but the differences are the basis of the synergy.
- Multiplying a godly legacy (Gen.1:28a). It takes both a father and a mother, who experience oneness with God and with each other, to properly raise children as God intends. Parents model their own roles to their children in the home. It affects the children's sexual identity. The parent who is the same-gender is the strongest role model a child has. And it affects future generations; we are raising the parents of our grandchildren. Receiving unconditional love from their parents based on a couple's oneness with each other is the greatest gift and best foundation for a child's life. They carry into life what they see at home - good and bad.

A godly marriage is opposed by Satan, who wants to destroy it - by deception and by temptation. He is a deceiver, a liar and a thief. His opposition is focused on independence from God, based on pride. Satan's success with the first married couple, Adam and Eve, resulted in:

- mankind spoiling the image of God through sin (Rom.3:23);
- marital companionship being threatened by blame and competition (Gen.3:12,16); and
- a godless legacy (Gen.4:8).

We need to realize that marriage takes place on a spiritual battlefield, not on a romantic balcony. Satan's power is threatened by couples who are becoming one, and so he concentrates his attacks on them. We need to see through the problem - my spouse is not the problem; Satan is behind it. We then need to join forces and resist him, to attack the problem, not each other.

God's Plan for Oneness

God's plan is that: a man should leave his parents; he should cleave to his wife; and they should become one flesh (Gen.2:24). In leaving the parents to cleave to each other, the parents are still to be honoured by their married children (although no longer necessarily to be obeyed). But over-dependence on parents after marriage creates problems. Children affect a marriage relationship when they arrive and when they leave. "Cleaving" means to establish a commitment to one another. Becoming one flesh means to establish intimacy.

Before Eve was created, Adam had an unmet need (even in his perfect circumstances). God said it wasn't good to be alone"; he was incomplete. God met the need by providing him with a wife. God showed him his need by bringing the animals together and showing him he was the only one without a mate. God "fashioned" (customized) Eve for Adam and presented her to him. Adam recognized her as being God's perfect provision for him, and he gladly received her (Gen.2:23). Therefore the basis of our acceptance of our mate is our faith in God's integrity. Adam focused on God's flawless character in what He provided, not on Eve's performance or his evaluation of her.

There are two barriers which make it difficult for us to receive our mate as a gift of God in this way: (a) our natural differences from each other and (b) our own natural weaknesses, both of which can make us critical of them. (There are 4 basic personality types: (a) dominant; (b) pleaser; (c) perfectionist; and (d) influencer.) God made Adam and Eve different from each other, but they were both made in the image of God. Differences are tools that God uses to cause us to rely on His power instead of our own. Weaknesses have divine purposes and should not be a basis for rejecting our mate. Rejecting our mate in any way is to reject

God's provision, and to fail in fulfilling His purpose and plan for our marriage. We need, as an act of our will, to accept our mate as God's personal gift, to meet our aloneness needs. We should not try to change them. We can only change ourselves.

The result of leaving, cleaving and becoming one flesh is transparency and openness with one another. It says that Adam and Eve were naked and were not ashamed. Showing our vulnerability encourages our mate's support. "A hurt that is shared diminishes; a hurt that is carried alone expands."

God's Power for Oneness

God has provided the power necessary to fulfill His purposes and plan for this oneness. We need to make God the source of our power. We experience this power by knowing God through Christ and allowing His Spirit to control our lives through faith. We were not created to "live the good life", but for the purpose of knowing God personally. God is more interested in our character than our comfort. Sin is what prevents us from knowing God. The Holy Spirit has been given to be our "helper", to teach us how to live by guiding us to truth, and to convict us of the presence of sin in our lives. He is the power to enable us to forgive each other when we are wronged, and to love each other unconditionally. Being "filled" with the Spirit does not mean we get more of God; it means He gets more of us. It results in us exhibiting the fruit of the Spirit.

We need to make a daily choice to love and submit to Christ (rather than our own way), to be honest with God about our sin, and to surrender areas of our life we have kept from Him.

Understanding Communications

In a marriage we need the communication skills of both listening and expressing (but not of course at the same time) in order to avoid misunderstandings. These take: (a) time and effort; (b) trustworthiness; and (c) transparency (complete personal and emotional openness). There are 5 possible communication levels we can engage in:

- the cliché level (non-sharing);
- the fact level (sharing what we know);
- the opinion level (sharing what we think);
- the emotion level (sharing what we feel); and
- transparency (sharing who we are).

As married couples we should be aiming for the higher levels.

The Importance of Listening

Listening is seeking to understand what's going on inside the other person. It's different from just hearing them. Thinking of a response inhibits real listening. Listening with empathy is looking beyond the words to the meaning and intent behind them. We should be 'interested', rather than trying to be 'interesting'. Poor listening habits stifle communication; these include:

- faking interest, while thinking about something else;
- selective listening (as the song goes: "Man hears only what he wants to hear, and disregards the rest."); and
- protective listening (ignoring threatening messages).

We need to "open our ears". We need to listen with an attitude of wanting to hear what God may be saying to us through our mate. We should ask questions and paraphrase back for clarification. We should not interrupt, or give advice, when what is needed is to acknowledge what is being said or felt. ("She wants my shoulder, not my head.") Listening encourages understanding and builds oneness. Don't jump too quickly to a solution when what is wanted is acknowledgement of feelings that are being expressed.

The Importance of Expressing

People bring into marriage varying patterns of expressiveness, on a range from completely cognitive (factual) expression to completely emotional (feelings). If a couple is at two different places on this spectrum it can lead to a lot of misunderstanding. Generally people have to deal with emotional issues before logic will prevail; being upset emotionally blocks cognitive thinking. We should allow our mate the freedom to use their own style of expressiveness, and yet attempt to speak to them in their language rather than our own.

Reluctance to express ourselves can come from various causes, such as childhood programming, a poor self-image and fear of rejection, pride (being "macho") or even from a false concept of spirituality.

Expressing ourselves involves the risk of being emotionally intimate. (Intimacy = "in-to-me-see".) None of us is married to a mind reader. We need to entrust ourselves to our mate for their understanding in order to strengthen the relationship. We need to be explicit about what we want and don't want. We need to express our thoughts, feelings and needs. We need to determine: (a) what we want to say; (b) how we want to say it; and (c) when is the best time to say it.

Sexual Intimacy

The purposes of sex in marriage are: (a) procreation; (b) pleasure; and (c) protection from temptation from outside. A satisfying sex life is the result of a satisfying marriage, not the reverse. A satisfying marriage results when a couple places value on creating (a) companionship (Greek: "philo"), (b) lasting commitment ("agape"); and (c) deepening passion ("eros"). These are the three New Testament words for love. The opposite condition is complacency, rejection and withdrawal. Sex is a thermometer that can measure our individual well-being and the health of our relationship.

Sex has three aspects. It is:

- physical (it can be affected by our health, fatigue, energy level, headaches, pregnancy, menopause, etc.);
- mental (it can be affected by stress, being preoccupied, and by incorrect information and fantasizing, such as is promoted by the media and by pornography); and
- emotional (it can be affected by abuse, unresolved anger and conflict, guilt feelings, and poor self-worth).

In sex, we should focus on the other person, not just on our own self-gratification. It is very harmful for us to say anything negative (even in joking) about our mate's body, and to make fun of them - in private or in public.

When companionship is lacking, sex can lose its meaning. When commitment is lacking (such as not being trustworthy, or not keeping our promises), sex can seem risky and vulnerable. When passion is lacking, sex can become routine and mechanical.

Sex in marriage can be improved by understanding gender differences. For example: Men tend to switch on more quickly (are more easily aroused); they are stimulated physically and visually; they need to feel respected; and their orgasms tend to be shorter and more intense. Women tend to warm up more slowly; they are stimulated more by the overall relationship and by touch; they need to feel needed and safe; are more easily distracted; and they have longer, more in-depth orgasms.

A sexual relationship can also be improved by building together:

- Companionship: by romantic times together; tenderness; and communication - having things to talk about (other than the children);
- Commitment: by being faithful and respectful, by forgiving,

and by being selfless; and

- Passion: by planning for times together, becoming a student of each other, and being creative (to promote variety).

Resolving Marital Conflict

The goal of marriage is not to be conflict-free (since that is impossible), but to handle conflict well when it occurs. Conflict often happens inadvertently, and by little things that we take offense at. Sometimes we can look back and be amazed at how little an issue started the whole thing.

Our choice of response will either drive us apart or bind us together. Possible responses include:

(a) yielding;

(b) withdrawing or avoiding;

(c) determining to win (which means "You end up going to bed with a loser"); or

(d) lovingly resolving it together, valuing the relationship more than the issue and being 'right'.

We can show anger when: (a) our "rights" have been violated; (b) our expectations have not been met; or (c) we have been hurt emotionally. As we saw earlier, anger is a symptom of an underlying hurt. If an argument is caused by anger, we need to discover and admit what's really wrong. We need to know why our anger can be so intense over something so relatively minor. We each need to know what makes us angry.

Anger can be a powerful weapon and can be very destructive (Gen.4:6,7). It needs to be controlled, or else it can result in: (a) bitterness; (b) depression; and (c) lack of spiritual joy. (Someone has said: "The most miserable people are carnal Christians; the Holy Spirit won't let them enjoy themselves."). Unresolved conflicts accumulate and can intensify future conflicts ("Enough bricks make a wall"). We can control our anger by: (a) getting the facts right; (b) learning to get angry slowly; and (c) staying on the issue, not the person.

A marriage can sadly degenerate into an insult-for-insult relationship. We can try to punish our mate by actions or words. This relationship is rooted in an unforgiving and hardened attitude. It focuses on "my rights" and "my feelings". ("Hurt people hurt people".) It is often characterized either by "hiding" (silence - "I don't want to talk about it", as a means of controlling the situation), or else by "hurling" words. But we have been called to be a blessing to each other (*"not returning evil for evil or reviling for reviling, but on the contrary blessing"* - 1 Pet.3:9). This involves responding kindly when we are offended. ("It takes 10 compliments to negate one negative statement.") (*"A soft answer turns away wrath, but a harsh word stirs up anger"* – Prov.15:1) It forgets about one-upmanship.

Resolving conflict requires loving confrontation. Much of the friction is caused by the tone of voice. We need to "speak the truth in love" (Eph.4:15). We should avoid bringing up the past. We should focus on just a single issue at a time. We should be gentle with each other. ("Nothing is as strong as gentleness, and nothing is as gentle as real strength."). We need to check our motivation - is it a desire for control or revenge, or rather for resolution? We also need to check the timing and setting of the confrontation (e.g. not in front of others).

We should focus on the person's behaviour, not their person. We should focus on "I" statements, not "you" statements (such as "how I feel when that happens"; rather than "you make me feel unhappy"). We should be prepared to accept confrontation, as well as give it. And we should try to agree on how to discuss future conflicts.

Resolving conflict requires forgiveness. The offender needs to be willing to admit they were wrong, be willing to say they are sorry (and mean it); and be willing to make amends, if possible. They should never take their forgiveness for granted. The offended person needs to grant unconditional forgiveness (Eph.4:32; Matt.18:21,22), and to forget. This allows the future to break from the past. Granting forgiveness is not denying or repressing the wrong or the resulting hurt. It is a conscious choice and surrender of our right to get even and is the beginning of the healing process. It should be done privately (first), specifically, generously and graciously.

It has been wisely said that "Marriage is the union of two good forgivers" and also that "Forgiveness involves setting the prisoner free and realizing that I'm the prisoner." Forgiveness is not a natural thing to do. We are most like God when we forgive. The process of reconciliation starts with forgiveness. If we are the offending person we should take the initiative. If we are the offended person should resist the natural tendency to rehearse the hurt. We should discuss specific solutions (e.g. "What do you need from me?"), and also what to change in order to prevent a recurrence. One person alone can forgive the other, but it takes both for reconciliation.

Counseling Engaged Couples or Newly-weds

Being able to counsel couples who are shortly to be married or are just married is extremely valuable, because it may help to prevent problems in the marriage in the future or, at the very least, help each party go into the marriage with their eyes open to the potential pitfalls. Some couples may have made the decision that they want to spend the rest of their lives with each other, but they may have not thought through all the implications of this step, nor all the areas of their lives that it will impact. Even if they have, they may not have considered these same areas from the other's point of view and not appreciate that they may be very different.

The counseling process enables the couple to talk to each other, particularly at a time when all the busyness of wedding preparations, and its aftermath, can be a distraction from what is really important – the health of their marriage. Appendix 3 includes a series of topics and questions for you to go through in person with the couple or, if this is not possible, for them to review themselves. These questions, along with a brief introduction to each topic, is contained in the book "Getting Married", which I wrote along with my wife, Sandra, and is available from the publisher, Hayes Press (www.hayespress.org).

21. THE SPECIAL COUNSELING ROLE OF ELDERS

Whereas other people in the church should not normally go around looking to intervene as a counselor, and so run the risk of becoming busybodies (1 Tim.5:13), overseers (also known as elders) sometimes need to take the initiative to be alert to those in their local church who need godly advice, encouragement, exhortation, admonition or discipline:

> *"we exhort you, brethren, warn those who are unruly, comfort the fainthearted, uphold the weak, be patient with all. See that no one renders evil for evil to anyone, but always pursue what is good both for yourselves and for all"* (1 Thess.5:14,15).

Local overseers are responsible to care for the church, as "shepherds", by "tending" (guiding) the "flock", and by "feeding" (teaching) them. Because of their role as "pastors", overseers have a particular need to be able to provide practical and wise scriptural counsel to those in their local assembly. It is therefore incumbent on all overseers to develop, by the enabling of God, an ability to do this well and to be approachable.

"Tend My sheep ... Feed My sheep" (Jn.21:16,17).

One of the incentives to do this is because they are accountable to care for the souls of those put under their charge: *"Obey those who rule over you, and be submissive, for they watch out for your souls, as those who must give account"* (Heb.13:17).

Because of their role, overseers must attempt to act in a way that is beyond reproach in their dealing with each person, regardless of how those people may in turn deal with them:

"a bishop must be blameless, as a steward of God, not self-willed, not quick-tempered, not given to wine, not violent, not greedy for money, but hospitable, a lover of what is good, sober-minded, just, holy, self-controlled, holding fast the faithful word as he has been taught, that he may be able, by sound doctrine, both to exhort and convict those who contradict" (Titus 1:7-9).

"The elders who are among you I exhort ... shepherd the flock of God which is among you, serving as overseers, not by compulsion but willingly ... nor as being lords over those entrusted to you, but being examples to the flock" (1 Pet.5:1-3).

"A bishop then must be ... able to teach ... gentle, not quarrelsome ... one who rules his own house well, having his children in submission with all reverence (for if a man does not know how to rule his own house, how will he take care of the church of God?" (1 Tim.3:2-7).

Policemen or Counsellors?

Overseers also have a responsibility for governing the assembly, to maintain the standards of God's house. This can sadly sometimes require intervening in a situation which requires them to recommend that discipline for a person in their local church for wrong-doing is carried out by the church. These two roles of counselor and disciplinarian can sometimes come into conflict, although it need not; it is comparable to the role of a father with his children. A father needs to both guide and discipline his children, and he does both out of love for them and a sincere desire for their good (and this comparison is used in 1 Tim.3:5). Sometimes however these two roles may appear to be incompatible. A brother or sister who is being offered counseling may not open up to an overseer, because of fear of discipline.

But, generally, during the stage where sinful behaviour is beginning to emerge, the primary opportunity is for counseling, not discipline, with a view to preventing the problem from escalating. But if the counsel is not heeded, and the sin requires it, the elders' responsibility is to act in discipline. Subsequently, however, if a repentant attitude is shown, they may again be able to act as counselors to help bring about recovery and restoration. In both cases, of course, the success will depend on the willingness of the person to respond to such counseling. Discipline is primarily required where the person is unwilling to heed the earlier counseling.

Discipline in the Church

Where discipline is required, overseers together have a unique responsibility, and they act on behalf of the church. With respect to the offender, discipline deals primarily with their attitude and is intended always to lead to repentance, if God grants it (2 Tim.2:25). Where there is a God-given spirit of repentance, counseling can then be used as a positive means to aid in recovery. Other purposes of discipline are:

(a) to prevent any recurrence of the sin;

(b) to warn others about such sin (1 Tim.5:20); and

(c) to preserve the testimony of God's people (2 Sam.12:14).

Discipline can take several forms, such as:

(a) private admonition;

(b) public admonition (with the assembly present);

(c) restriction on service (which is normally advised to the assembly); and

(d) excommunication.

In the case of excommunication, and restoration, the elders commend it to the assembly; it is the assembly who carry it out (1 Cor.5:13). In other cases, it is the elders who carry it out.

Acting Together

When an overseer is attempting to counsel someone in the church, he is usually acting as an individual. All information is therefore kept confidential and is only shared with other overseers with the person's permission. The exception to this is where a matter comes to light that require overseers' united action, such as discipline. In that case the brother or sister would be advised that it has become an oversight matter. When overseers are investigating the need for discipline, they must: (a) take care to limit the matter to as few people as possible (Matt.18:15-17); and (b) keep it confidential from others. Others in the church should therefore not know that the matter is being dealt with unless and until any public announcement needs to be made.

When overseers make decisions, they do so collectively. The authority of overseers is collective and is not vested in any one of them. To show this collectivity, interviews regarding such matters as reception into the assembly and discipline normally involve more than one overseer. When decisions need to be made about dealing with a brother or sister in the assembly, the overseers need to reach agreement on the course of action. Where a family member is being dealt with, the related overseer should normally not take an active part in the decision, other than providing pertinent information that he may be aware of. Finally, it is not for those in the church to pass judgment on the manner in which overseers carry out their work. They are responsible to their overseers, and each overseer is responsible to the Lord.

"We urge you, brethren, to recognize those who labor among you, and are over you in the Lord and admonish you" (1 Thess. 5:12).

"Obey those who rule over you, and be submissive" (Heb.13:17).

22. THE EMMAUS EXAMPLE

"His name will be called ... Counselor" (Is.9:6).

Now behold, two of them were traveling that same day to a village called Emmaus, which was about seven miles from Jerusalem. And they talked together of all these things which had happened. So it was, while they conversed and reasoned, that Jesus Himself drew near and went with them. But their eyes were restrained, so that they did not know Him. And He said to them, "What kind of conversation is this that you have with one another as you walk and are sad?" Then the one whose name was Cleopas answered and said to Him, "Are You the only stranger in Jerusalem, and have You not known the things which happened there in these days?"

And He said to them, "What things?" So they said to Him, "The things concerning Jesus of Nazareth, who was a Prophet mighty in deed and word before God and all the people, and how the chief priests and our rulers delivered Him to be condemned to death, and crucified Him. But we were hoping that it was He who was going to redeem Israel. Indeed, besides all this, today is the third day since these things happened. Yes, and certain women of our company, who arrived at the tomb early, astonished us. When they did not find His body, they came saying that they had also seen a vision of angels who said He was alive.

And certain of those who were with us went to the tomb and found it just as the women had said; but Him they did not see." Then He said to them, "O foolish ones, and slow of heart to believe in all that the prophets have spoken! Ought not the Christ to have suffered these things and to enter into His glory?" And beginning at Moses and all the Prophets, He expounded to them in all the Scriptures the things concerning Himself.

Then they drew near to the village where they were going, and He indicated that He would have gone farther. But they constrained Him, say-

ing, "Abide with us, for it is toward evening, and the day is far spent." And He went in to stay with them. Now it came to pass, as He sat at the table with them, that He took bread, blessed and broke it, and gave it to them. Then their eyes were opened and they knew Him; and He vanished from their sight. And they said to one another, "Did not our heart burn within us while He talked with us on the road, and while He opened the Scriptures to us?" So they rose up that very hour and returned to Jerusalem, and found the eleven and those who were with them gathered together, saying, "The Lord is risen indeed, and has appeared to Simon!" And they told about the things that had happened on the road, and how He was known to them in the breaking of bread."

The two who were walking down the road from Jerusalem to Emmaus that day, as described in Luke 24, were very emotionally upset - and it showed. It could be seen on their faces and in their walk. It was resurrection day, but they didn't know it. They didn't know the man who joined them. And yet, at the end of their encounter with Him, their mood had totally changed, their hearts were "burning" and, despite how late it was, they hurried back uphill the seven miles to Jerusalem. It was indeed a successful counseling session by the master counselor. Yet their circumstances hadn't changed. What did Jesus do and say that made all the difference in their outlook?

(a) He Joined Them in Their Activity

"Jesus Himself drew near and went with them." (Lk.24:15) it says. Rather than confronting them head-on and stopping them in their tracks, He joined in walking with them and in their conversation. Our counseling opportunities may occur in various ways. Sometimes we can become involved through invitation, perhaps by being asked for advice. Sometimes, however, we may take the initiative because we sense there is a difficulty, and we feel led to offer assistance. However it is that we become involved, the initial approach is critical so that the other person

is encouraged to accept your help. Direct confrontation may be tempting, but it is seldom the appropriate means to use. He just joined in their activity.

(b) He Used Questions to Draw Them Out

"He said to them, "What kind of conversation is this that you have with one another as you walk and are sad?" (24:17). Counseling is not telling people what to do; it is helping them through conversation to discover it for themselves. It is helping them realize and be convinced of the underlying cause of their problem, and what they need to do about it. Good questions, asked in the right way, are usually the best way to do this, and questioning is a skill that can be learned. Even when the two on the Emmaus road answered with a question of their own, Jesus continued with another question, probing for details - *"What things?"* (24:19). The details are always important, because they reveal the thinking that underlies the feelings.

(c) He Addressed Their Emotional State First

"What kind of conversation is this that you have with one another as you walk and are sad?" (24:17). He asked them why they were feeling the way they were. Emotions are a clue to the underlying problem, but they are not the problem itself. Telling someone to "not feel that way" is not usually helpful. Focusing on their emotional state first allowed them to express what they were feeling, which is usually necessary before trying to think of a solution. Sufficient time is generally required to acknowledge people's emotional state before they can reason out a solution; negative emotions act as a block on our rational processes.

(d) He Got Them to State the Thinking and Beliefs That Were at the Root of Their Feelings

"We were hoping that it was He who was going to redeem Israel" (24:21). What people think and believe to be true determines both their behav-

iour and their emotional reactions to their circumstances. True counseling must penetrate to this level of belief, and so of necessity involve
some teaching of biblical truth. This requires much more than just trying to make someone feel better or exhorting them to behave differently. When people do in fact change their thinking (which is not at all
easy to do), their behaviour and emotional reactions inevitably change.
Generally people only change their underlying thinking and beliefs
when they themselves choose to do so, and in response to some strong
stimulus.

(e) He Then Revealed the Reality About the Situation, From Scripture, in Order to Change Their Thinking

*"O foolish ones, and slow of heart to believe in all that the prophets have
spoken! Ought not the Christ to have suffered these things and to enter into
His glory?"* (24:25,26). He challenged their false expectations. Then He
began to show them the truth of the situation, what was really happening, as revealed in God's Word - *"beginning at Moses and all the
Prophets, He expounded to them in all the Scriptures the things concerning Himself."* (24:27). The end result was that their hearts began to
"burn within" them (24:32) as He showed them what the scriptures
had to say about Himself. Their understanding was totally altered. He
could have revealed Himself right at the outset, but He wanted them to
learn the process of deriving it from the scriptures.

(f) When His Work Was Done, He Left

"He vanished from their sight" (24:31). Once the problem was solved,
he did not prolong it, which could have complicated matters. He left
them. And not only did this counseling encounter overcome their
problem, they had also received a wonderful insight into the person of
the Lord Jesus.

What a wonderful example to follow!

APPENDIX 1: A BRIEF HISTORY OF PSYCHOLOGY

The main aim of psychology is to predict human behaviour by studying the mind. By first studying healthy minds, clinical psychology is used in particular to treat people with illnesses of the mind. Mental illness includes such things as depression (which is a mood disorder which involves a perpetual sense of hopelessness and lethargy), anxiety disorders, obsessive-compulsive disorders and schizophrenia (distortion of reality).

Psychology came after psychiatry. A psychiatrist is a medical doctor who is specially trained to treat the mind, and who is able to prescribe medications. Psychology research has progressed over the years from relying on mere introspection to studying the structures of the mind (memory, perception, etc.), then to studying human behaviour, and more recently to a more objective study of the inner mind. Following are some of the more significant developments over the years in theories of psychology.

Experimental psychology began in the late 1800's, based on the study of the nervous system. Analogies were made with neurology – the study of electricity. 1879 is taken as the beginning of the discipline of psychology, when a German, Wilhelm Wundt set up a lab in Leipzig. The first PhD in psychology was awarded in 1881. Wundt continued researching for 60 years, almost half the total time period psychology has been a recognized science. Charles Darwin also had an influence; his theories implied that intelligence and instinct were not fundamentally different, and put humans within the realm of materialistic science. Francis Galton (also from England) theorized that psychological qualities were inherited. In the U.S. William James at Harvard was effectively the founder of applied psychology and its popularization. Research in the U.S. was generally less structured than in Europe.

167

Psychoanalysis

Sigmund Freud developed his methods of psychoanalysis in the 19th century. He divided the mind into three parts: the id (fundamental urges for food, warmth affection and sex), the ego (which deals with reality) and the superego (which he said contains the moral standards inculcated by society). He said the three parts compete for a fixed amount of mental energy. As a child develops, he claimed the id is satisfied through different parts of the body. Conflicts with what the environment provides are resolved in ways that determines the person's basic personality traits. He believed that ideas could lodge in the subconscious and be transformed into bodily symptoms. There is no experimental evidence, however, for these parts of the mind or for his theories.

Classical psychoanalysis is based on the idea that a neurotic anxiety is the reaction of the ego when a previously repressed id impulse wants to be expressed. The past childhood event which repressed it must be uncovered so that it can be addressed in light of adult reality. The repression can then be lifted by techniques such as free association (saying whatever comes into your mind) and dream analysis, both of which can take a long time. In both cases the therapist interprets what is said. If the patient denies the interpretation, it is taken as a sign that it is in fact correct. However, this results in a practical problem: how does the therapist know that 'no' is really 'yes'?

Transference neurosis is a crucial part of the treatment, where the patient reaches the stage where they express emotions towards the therapist that they actually feel towards other persons. The therapist should not say anything helpful as this might deflect the patient's own effort to uncover the repressed conflicts.

Freud began working in Vienna with neuroses, rather than organic problems. He started experimenting with hypnosis. By 1940 his writings provided the basic concepts for clinical psychology and personality theory. His theories did away with rationality; it produced a discrepancy between what people thought their motivations were and what they really were. Many psychologists have deep reservations about psychoanalysis, since it relies on a theory with no supporting evidence, and involves treatments which seem quite counter-intuitive.

Physiological Therapy

Some mental illnesses came to be regarded primarily as physical problems in the brain which need therefore to be treated by drugs or surgery (sometimes supplemented by relaxation therapy, for example). Depression for example may result from failure of certain neural transmitters. Schizophrenia is generally regarded to be affected by heredity. Mental illness is often regarded as the result of a predisposition plus a trigger that activates it.

Behavioural Therapy

The next development focused on understanding human behaviour. This is based on 'stimulus and response' – how people react to various stimuli. Research has been undertaken on learning and unlearning through conditioned responses, which is used today for example in advertising. Therapies include counter-conditioning, systematic desensitizing, modeling, role-playing, rewarding, etc. The beginnings of behaviouralism, around 1900, came from the study of animals. It denied that any actual 'thinking' was going on, only a mechanistic response to stimuli. It had the effect of taking control away from the mind and into the environment. For example, John Watson said there was no mind in psychology; 'mind' is not a scientific entity. Later B.F. Skinner developed behaviouralism to its height. By 1950 behaviouralism controlled most research.

Cognitive Therapy

Meanwhile there was increasing dissent by cognitive psychologists, reinforced by the advance of computer programming. It insisted that the mind is real and does something. Cognitive therapy focuses on what happens between the stimulus and the response – how people acquire, store and use information. Thoughts are considered to be what causes feelings; therefore changing the thoughts can change the feelings. It doesn't concern itself particularly with the origin of the problem, but only with the present solution. It is often combined with aspects behavioural therapy.

Thoughts and beliefs cannot be changed instantly. They must be consciously identified, and consistently and frequently challenged in order to change. This method gives the therapist a more directive role, which of course introduces the risk of therapist bias. It can involve discovering 'automatic negative thoughts' in order to replace them with neutral or positive thoughts.

Humanistic Therapy

Self-help therapy has become popular. It assumes that people are basically healthy and good (which denies the intrinsically selfish nature of people), with an innate drive for growth and self-actualization. (Carl Rogers was one of the leaders of this movement and gave rise to "Rogerian therapy"). It tries to help them "get in touch with" their true feelings and learn to express them regardless of what others might think. The therapist always must give unconditional positive regard to the patient. Since the patient must take responsibility for himself or herself, the therapist must not give advice. Rogers assumed that success in therapy depended largely on the therapist's empathy, genuineness and warmth. The main problem with this approach is that it is demonstrably flawed. People often want to do selfish things, which don't make them happy or good citizens.

The Development of Applied Psychology

Psychology as a treatment began later than psychiatry. Originally only psychiatrists treated the mentally ill. They generally saw it as a disease of the nervous system, to be treated by diet or rest. Then treatment became more invasive – drugs, shock treatment and surgery (e.g. frontal lobotomies). Gradually psychologists were introduced in a supportive role. As a result, other causal factors began to be considered, such as family problems, economic security, etc. World War II gave prominence to psychologists who provided counseling to returning soldiers. Intelligence and personality tests became common for employment purposes – the development of industrial and organizational psychology.

There was increasing tension between the MD psychiatrists, who had no research qualifications, and the PhD psychologists, who were more academically qualified but lower in rank in practicing with patients. Another result of the combination was more diverse therapies. It continued to be materialistic, however, denying anything that couldn't be explained by a physical mechanism, such as the human soul and spirit.

Christian Beliefs and Psychology

Christian beliefs are sometimes explained away by psychologists as being just coping mechanisms (a 'wish-fulfillment') This cannot of course be proven (or disproved) by laboratory experiments. Psychology assumes the doctrine of God's non-existence, because it wants it that way. Some psychologists regard Christian faith as contributing to their patients' neuroses. Some psychological theories are contrary to Christianity (e.g. Carl Rogers – humans are fundamentally good). Psychology students are often taught that psychology (like science) has 'disproved' old-fashioned beliefs like Christianity. However, all psychology can do is study what the mind is like now. There is however no inherent incompatibility between Christianity and true psychology. The Christian realizes that God makes the structures of the mind, and that psychology on its own provides an incomplete understanding. The study of how mankind operates is a good thing, and it should bring glory to God.

Any integration of psychology with Christianity needs to recognize that humans are created beings, created for a purpose and in the image of God. Our minds work the way they do to serve that purpose; they have flaws because we rebel against those purposes. Any integration that does away with the reality of sin and evil is not really integration. The fact of human sinfulness can be studied empirically, but why that is so is a matter of revelation, not psychology.

APPENDIX 2: CASE STUDY & REVIEW

Bill has been worried for some time about Jack's spiritual life and seeming lack of interest in assembly things. He has been trying to build a good relationship with Jack by paying attention to him, being interested in what's going on in his life, and helping him with things he needed doing. But he wants to be able to counsel Jack to help him reach a higher level in his life and service for God. And so one day he arranges to have lunch with him. Here is the conversation that took place over lunch *{Bill's strategy noted in italics].*

Bill: Hi, Jack. It's good to see you. Thanks for agreeing to get together for a bite. How's your day going? *[an ice-breaker]*

Jack: Not bad. My buddy called in sick so I'm pretty busy right now.

Bill: Are you enjoying working at the store? *[moving from facts to feelings]*

Jack: It's not too bad. I don't like the evenings and weekends, but the pay's pretty good. I'm trying to save up to go back to school and get a degree.

Bill: What do you want to do – do you have a particular career in mind? *[probe for specifics]*

Jack: Yeah, sort of. I've been thinking about getting into graphic design. It looks quite interesting.

Bill: I guess being in your mid-twenties is when you're at the stage where you'd like to figure out where you're going in life. *[use the opening to zero in on life goals]*

Jack:Yes I would. Getting 'old", I guess. I'd like to settle down and get into something.

Bill:Jack how do you feel about your role in the assembly right now? Are you OK with it? *[change of topic – to assembly life]*

Jack:I figured you'd bring that up. I don't really have a role right now. I don't have any close friends there, and, I don't know, I just don't seem to fit in.

Bill:How long is it since you were baptized? Six or seven years? *[take him back to his personal commitment, but in a non-threatening way]*

Jack: Oh...it must be about eight years now. But our assembly doesn't seem to be doing anything much. People are always complaining about things, and some of them seem kind of phony.

Bill:Is that why we don't see much of you at the meetings? *[link his comment to his behaviour]*

Jack:I go...sometimes. But I guess I'm not really that motivated. The people get to me sometimes. I don't really know them all that well.

Bill:Would you like to know them better? *[turn the problem to an aspiration]*

Jack:Yeah...some of them. They just seem so busy and wrapped up in their own lives. I don't feel very motivated to spend a lot of time with them.

Bill:Is there anyone in particular you have a problem with? *[probe for specifics]*

Jack:(Pause) Well, yeah. I don't have much time for Mr. Dermot. I know he's an overseer and everything, but I know what he's really like.

Bill: What do you mean? *[probe for more details]*

Jack: Well, just between you and me, when I was a lot younger, he was always putting me down and bossing me around. He was my Bible class teacher, and I guess he wanted to prove he was always right. And he was pretty mean to my parents. I got pretty upset at him a lot of times, but I just shut up.

Bill: Are you still upset at him? *[relate his answer to his present feelings]*

Jack: I don't think about it much any more but...yeah, I guess I am. When I'm at the hall and I see him, it kinda turns me off. But who's going to listen to me over him?

Bill: Have you ever tried talking to him about it? *[explore past attempts at resolution]*

Jack: I mentioned it once, but he just dismissed it. I didn't get anywhere. So, if that's the way he wants to be...

Bill: It sounds like there's still quite a bit of anger there. But, Jack, how are you getting along with the Lord these days? *[solidify the problem feeling, then change the topic – to personal spiritual life]*

Jack: Uh (pause)...not that great really. I know I ought to be reading my Bible and praying a lot, but I'm pretty hit and miss. Every once in a while I get enthusiastic, but then it wears off.

Bill: Would you like things to be different? Would you like to be a lively Christian? Is that something that is important to you. *[move from problem to aspiration]*

Jack: Yes, I really would. But I'm not sure how to go about it. Every time I try, I just fail, so I get back into my rut.

Bill: Jack, I would very much like to try to help you get out of that rut. Living as a true Christian is the most fulfilling and important thing there is. I'd love to see you really devote yourself to the Lord, and let Him show you what He could do with your life. You have a lot to give, you know. You're good with people, you know how to talk to them, and you're a very genuine person. Would you be willing to let me work with you on this? *[inspire him with real benefits of making a change, and offer support]*

Jack: What do you have in mind? What would we do?

Bill: I'm not exactly sure yet. I want to think about it. But I am willing if you are to get together on a regular basis and talk about it. We could do some Bible study together, pray about stuff going on in our lives, do things for the Lord together – things like that. How does that sound? *[note hesitancy; move gently to explore an action plan, based on the personal relationship]*

Jack: Yeah...that would be good. I'd be willing to give it a shot. I'm kind of in the doldrums these days, and I don't like it.

Bill: And about this matter of you and Mr. Dermot. I really think that's a big stumbling block in your spiritual life. I really think you need to get it resolved, and Id be willing to help you with that. *[bring back the unresolved issue, to explore a way forward]*

Jack: What do you have in mind?

Bill: I think it's important that you tell Mr. Dermot how you feel about the way he's been treating you. He may be totally surprised, or he may try to justify himself. I don't know. But I think it's important for you to tell him. And then you need to tell him you have forgiven him and, as far as you are concerned, it's over. *[prescribe a scripturally-sound specific action plan]*

Jack:I'm not sure I'd look forward to that. What if he doesn't admit it?

Bill:You can't control that. You can't let that determine whether or not you put this problem behind you, or else you'll be a captive to it for a long time. *[clarify that forgiveness doesn't depend on others' actions; reinforce his need to act]*

Jack:But I'm not sure I feel like forgiving him.

Bill:I don't doubt it. But forgiveness is a choice. The Bible tells us in Ephesians to forgive each other just as God in Christ forgave us. What He forgave us for is a lot more than this. *[clarify that feelings should not dictate our actions]*

Jack:Yeah, that's for sure. O.K. I'll certainly think about that. I'm tired of feeling this way. It's time to get on with things.

Bill:That's exactly the right way to think about it, Jack. So, why don't we agree to meet once a week for the next two months. What time's good for you? *[move towards specific arrangements]*

Jack:Well, Thursday and Friday evenings are out because of work. Any other evening's good.

Bill:Well that leaves Monday or Tuesday during the week, because Wednesday's the prayer meeting. How about we do it every Monday. Where? Your place or mine? I'll come to your place – it's quieter. *[establish own commitment to attend the assembly meetings; nail down details]*

Jack:O.K.

Bill:That's great. We'll start this Monday – say 7:30. And we'll talk some more about your meeting with Mr. Dermot. Would you like some more coffee? *[once finalized, get closure and change the subject before he changes his mind]*

CASE STUDY REVIEW

Was this a successful counseling session? Why?

This was a successful session. Bill helped Jack to honestly examine his behaviour and his thinking. They came up with a specific and Biblical action plan, and arranged follow-up.

What were the symptoms of Jack's problem?

Lack of interest in spiritual things and assembly meetings.

What was the underlying problem?

Primarily his grudge against Mr. Dermot, and the resulting alienation from others in the assembly which deprived him of support for his spiritual growth.

What did Bill do well and not so well?

He kept the conversation on course, moved easily into spiritual matters, was not too directive, probed for the deeper issues, and proposed a workable action plan. He didn't get into a critique of Mr. Dermot, but kept the focus on what Jack needed to do.

Did Bill confront Jack at any point? How did he do it?

A little bit, such as by challenging Jack directly about his role in the assembly and his lack of attendance, he pressed him on the need to confront Mr. Dermot and to forgive him unconditionally.

APPENDIX 3: COUNSELING QUESTIONS FOR NEWLYWEDS AND THOSE TO BE MARRIED

1. THE FUNDAMENTALS OF MARRIAGE

1. Read Genesis 2:18-24. Why was Eve initially created?
2. How did Eve lose her equal status and become subject to her husband Adam? (Genesis 3:16, 12, 16; 1 Timothy 2:11-15)
3. How does the physical union of marriage relate to where Eve's body came from?
4. What was the effect of "the fall" on Adam's position? (Genesis 3:16-19; 1 Timothy 2:12-15)
5. Read 1 Corinthians 11:3-12. What does it mean *that "the head of the woman is the man"*?
6. Read Ephesians 5:22-33. What does the marriage of a man and woman symbolize spiritually?
7. What is a husband's responsibility to his wife?
8. Read 1 Corinthians 13:1-8,13. For the husband-to-be, what aspect of love do you think will be the most difficult?
9. What is a wife's responsibility to her husband?
10. Why do you think this is?
11. To what extent can you disagree with someone and still be subject to them?
12. From Matthew 19:6 and 1 Corinthians 7:39, how long is marriage for?
13. What is God's attitude to divorce? (Malachi 2:16)

2. FEELINGS, EMOTIONS, GOALS AND NEEDS

1. What is the goal of your marriage relationship?
2. What are your built-in personal needs?

3. How can these basic needs be fully met:
   a. by ignoring them?
   b. by seeking satisfaction in achievement or status?
   c. by other peoples' recognition of your worth?
   d. by my spouse's behaviour toward me?
   e. by the Lord?
   f. by another way?
4. How does Colossians 2:10 help you to understand how you should respond to situations that may occur in your marriage relationship?
5. How do you react inside when your fiancé says or does something that makes you feel somewhat rejected or put down?
6. How do you tend to react when your fiancé shares a negative feeling they have had, which is based on something you said or did? Does this encourage or discourage future sharing? Why?
7. How can you each learn to express negative feelings without becoming defensive, avoiding them, or becoming angry (and so "shutting down" or "lashing out")?
8. What is the difference between a goal and a desire (as the words are used above)? What action does each call for?
9. What plans do you have for working together for the Lord?
10. In what specific ways can you help each other's spiritual development?
11. What does Ephesians 4:32 mean to you that you are *to "forgive just as Christ has forgiven you"*?
12. In every circumstance in our relationships, we choose (consciously or unconsciously) to manipulate or else to minister. Explain the difference and what lies behind each of these.
13. "Agape" is the Greek word used in the original New Testament for the love that we should have for each other, and that comes

from God. Husbands are especially mentioned, such as in Ephesians 5:25 and Romans 13:8. What is "agape" love? What other kinds are there? (Clue: the words are "phileo and "eros".).

3. UNDERSTANDING YOUR RELATIONSHIP

1. How relatively important in a marriage relationship do you think the following are:
   a. sexual attraction?
   b. having common interests?
   c. talking with each other?
2. In your relationship, who does most of the talking?
3. Are you a good listener? How do you show it?
4. Do you have any difficulty in talking about intimate things?
5. Are either of you moody?
6. How do you support each other's different temperaments?
7. How do each of you react when you're angry (shout, go silent, get even, etc.)?
8. What things tend to get you angry at each other?
9. How do you become reconciled, and who tends to give in first?
10. In 1 Corinthians 13:5 it says that love "*keeps no record of wrongs*". What does this mean?
11. In Ephesians 4:26, what does "*don't let the sun go down on your wrath*" mean?
12. What annoying habits does your fiancé have? How do you deal with them? Have you ever talked about these with each other?
13. Do you presently read the Bible and pray together regularly? (If not, would you like to?)
14. In what ways are both your temperaments alike and in what ways are they different?
15. To what extent do the following descriptions amply to you,

and to your partner:
  a. Moody
  b. Uptight
  c. Possessive
  d. A spender
  e. Rigid
  f. Calm
  g. Happy
  h. Stubborn
  i. Consistent
  j. Controlling
  k. Communicative
  l. Active
16. What are your fiancé's greatest emotional needs?
17. Husbands, what would you do if you came home one evening and you found your wife in tears, or a note saying she'd gone home to mother?

4. SPENDING TIME

1. How much of your free time do you expect to spend together?
2. How much a part of your time will church activities have (be specific)?
3. If your partner chose to (or had to) spend a lot of evenings working or taking courses, would this be a problem?
4. Do you both plan to work when you get married?
5. What time do you each go to bed and get up?
6. What do you do to relax?
7. Describe your ideal vacation.
8. What do you like to do as soon as you get home from work?
9. How should each of you share the household chores (be specific)?
10. How much time do you spend watching television? What

shows do you watch?

5. SPENDING MONEY

1. If you were each given $10,000 (£5000), how would you want to spend it?
2. What kind of financial records do you intend to keep? Who will keep them?
3. Have either of you kept personal financial records before?
4. Will you budget? How much detail will your budget have?
5. How much do you plan to put away in savings each month?
6. Will you expect to discuss and agree on larger purchases before one of you makes them?
7. Will you have separate or joint bank accounts?
8. Who will your salary belong to after you're married?
9. How much of your joint income do you plan to give to the Lord?
10. How often do you expect to eat out?
11. How much spending will be on gifts to other people (such as for Christmas and birthdays)?
12. Do you plan to go "all out" on each other at Christmas and birthdays, or keep it small?
13. What do you think should be the maximum in relation to your income that you should be in debt?
14. Where do you plan to keep important documents?
15. When do you expect to buy a house, or will you rent?
16. How long do you both expect to work to earn income?

6. SEX

1. Read Hebrews 13:4. What does "being faithful" mean to you?
2. Is it wrong to be attracted to a person other than your mate?
3. Do you plan to have a physical check-up before your wedding?

(We strongly suggest it)
4. Read 1 Corinthians 7:3-5. How often do you think it is usual for a couple to make love?
5. Are there times when you would expect not to have sex (such as during a menstrual period, late stages of pregnancy, etc.)?
6. What do you expect your reaction will be if your partner says "not tonight"?
7. Have you read a good educational book on sex together?
8. Is there anything you're a bit afraid of?
9. Is there a married couple you know that you would like to talk to about some of these things?
10. How important is showing affection before and after intercourse, and apart from intercourse?
11. Which do you say more often: "I love you", or "do you love me?"?
12. What kind of birth control, if any, do you intend to use? And why?
13. Have you done any research to support your decision?
14. For how long do you expect to use birth control?

7. RELATIONSHIPS

1. How do you feel about past boy/girl friends of your fiancé?
2. What part of your life do you expect other friends (of the same sex) to have, after you're married?
3. Do you plan to have a regular "night out with the boys/girls"?
4. How do you get along with your future in-laws?
5. How often do you expect to visit with your future in-laws and be visited by them?
6. How do you expect your relationship to change with your parents after you're married?
7. How would you feel if your in-laws wanted to move in with you?

8. Do you understand why your parents want things done a certain way at your wedding and reception? How receptive are you?

8. FAMILY LIFE

1. Do you plan to start a family? If so, when?
2. How many children would you like to have?
3. How close together in age would you like them?
4. How disappointed would you be if you found you were unable to have children of your own?
5. How do you feel about adopting children?
6. How much entertaining do you expect to do in your new home?

Did you love *Christian Counseling - How to Help Yourself and Others Live Biblically*? Then you should read *Our Spiritual Journey* by Keith Dorricott!

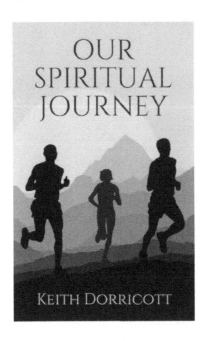

In this practical and Bible-based book, Keith Dorricott outlines a journey that God wants every Christian to embark upon, one that involves our own spirit and the Holy Spirit and that can result in a final destination of victorious Christian living!

1. The Journey of Spirituality
2. Understanding How God Made Us
3. From Before the Cradle to Beyond the Grave
4. Being Spiritual, Not Fleshly
5. Becoming Dead to Sin
6. Putting Off the Old
7. Confessing and Repenting
8. Communing With God

Also by Keith Dorricott

The Eternal Purpose: God's Master Plan for the Ages
Our Spiritual Journey
Christian Counseling - How to Help Yourself and Others Live Biblically

Made in the USA
Coppell, TX
13 May 2022

77754618R10109